A Manual of
Basic Bookkeeping

A MANUAL OF BASIC BOOKKEEPING

Principles + Practice

John Kellock, C.A., F.C.C.A., F.A.A.I., M.B.I.M.

Bell & Hyman
London

First published in 1981 by

Bell & Hyman Limited
Denmark House
37–39 Queen Elizabeth Street
London SE1 2QB

Designed by
Sue McDonald

Kellock, John
    A manual of basic bookkeeping.
    1. Bookeeping
    I. Title
657'.2   HF 5635

ISBN 0 7135 1285

Printed and bound in Great Britain
at The Pitman Press, Bath

Contents

Preface

This manual of bookkeeping presents the essential principles
of the subject for those taking their first course in bookkeeping. The method of presentation used is particularly
simple to follow, aids understanding, and also makes the book
easy to use for reference purposes. The book offers an introduc-
tory course in bookkeeping which is complete in itself or it
can be used to complement a traditional text.

The book includes:

- a *summary of the essential points* of each topic
- *simple instructions* on how to enter business transactions in
  the bookkeeping records
- easy to follow *examples* to illustrate each topic
- a series of *questions* to test the student's appreciation of
  each topic covered
- abbreviated *answers* to the computational type questions
- *a fully worked example* of the recording of business transactions up to and including Trading Profit and Loss
  Account and Balance Sheet
- a section on *Value Added Tax* showing how it is treated in
  the books of a business
- a *glossary* of some of the more common bookkeeping
  terms
- a *quick guide* to the basic bookkeeping entries.

The questions in the book are only given to test the student's
basic understanding of each topic as it is anticipated that
teachers and lecturers will prefer to use their own questions to
suit students' needs and level of course of study.
The manual will prove helpful to those students who find
difficulty with the more traditional type of text as the presentation directs the student to the key elements of each topic.
Also the presentation of the material should assist the lecturer
in lesson preparation.

John Kellock

To the Student

This manual will assist you in understanding the basic principles and practice of bookkeeping.

The manual's advantages are that:
- the key points of each topic are summarized in an easy to follow manner
- it will make the study of bookkeeping more enjoyable and less tedious for you
- the layout of the material allows you to *revise* the essential points quickly and easily
- questions are included relating to each section of the book to make it possible for you to test your understanding
- abbreviated answers are also given to most questions
- the manual is a complete guide to bookkeeping or it can be used to complement a textbook
- a quick guide to bookkeeping entries is included
- the simple indexing method makes the manual ideal for use as a reference book.

Business Transactions

Purpose

A business transaction is any exchange or transfer of goods or services which have a money value and for which an accounting entry must be made.
Example
On June 8 A. Draper sells goods value £100 to B. Black.

Two-fold Aspect

Each Business Transaction has a Two-fold Aspect
A. Draper has the following business transactions:
1 He buys for cash goods value £200.
2 He sells for cash goods value £100.
3 He pays electricity bill amounting to £20.

Analysis of Two-fold Aspect of each Transaction

Business Receives (Goods and services)	Business Gives (Goods and services)
1 Goods value £200	1 Cash value £200
2 Cash value £100	2 Goods value £100
3 Electricity value £20	3 Cash value £20

Types

Cash transaction
Settlement of the transaction takes place immediately.
Example
A. Draper buys goods for *Cash £200*

Credit transaction
Settlement of the amount due takes place at a later date.
Example
A. Draper buys goods on *Credit* for £100 from A. Smith.

Recording Cash Transactions

Purpose

To record transactions where settlement takes place immediately.

Basic Accounting System

. An account is opened to record each *aspect* of a transaction. Left hand side (Debit or DR) records *value received*. Right hand side (Credit or CR) records *value* given.
. Each account has a heading e.g. Electricity Account.
. This system of recording business transactions is known as *double-entry accounting*.
. Each account has a reference known as a *folio*.

Instructions

. Analyse each transaction as shown.
. Open an account for each aspect of transaction.
. Record value received on Debit side.
. Record value given on Credit side.

Example

Recording Cash Transactions in Accounts
A. Draper has the following transactions:
1 He pays into the business in cash *£1,000* as his capital.
2 He buys for cash goods value *£300*.
3 He sells goods for cash value *£200*.
4 He pays cash for office desk *£50*.

Note

The operation of transferring entries from one account to another is referred to as *'posting'*.

Illustration of an Account — Simplified Form

DR	Electricity Account	CR

This form is used to record entries where insufficient detail is given.

Detailed Form

DR				Electricity Account			CR
Date	Details	Folio	Amount	Date	Details	Folio	Amount

Cash Transactions recorded in Account Form
(Solution to Example on page 2)

DR		Cash Account		CR
Capital	(1)	£1,000	Purchases (2)	£300
Sales	(3)	200	Office desk (4)	50

DR	Capital Account	CR*	DR*	Purchases Account	CR
	Cash (1)	£1,000*	Cash (2)	£300*	

DR	Sales Account	CR	DR	Office Desk Account	CR
	Cash (3)	£200	Cash (4)	£50	

*The amount of £300 appearing on the Purchases Account is considered as a debit balance.
*The amount of £1,000 appearing on the Capital Account is considered as a credit balance.

Analysis of each transaction in above example

Value Received		Value Given	
1. Cash from owner	£1,000	1. Credit to capital	£1,000
2. Goods	£ 300	2. Cash	£ 300
3. Cash	£ 200	3. Goods	£ 200
4. Office desk	£ 50	4. Cash	£ 50

Recording Credit Transactions

Purpose

To record transactions when settlement takes place at a later date.

Basic Accounting System

. An Account is opened to record each *aspect* of a transaction.
. Each Account has two sides.
. Left hand side (Debit or DR) records *value received.*
. Right hand side (Credit or CR) records *value given.*
. Each Account has a heading e.g. *Purchases Account.*
. This system of recording business transactions is known as Double-entry Accounting.
. Each Account has a reference as a folio.

Instructions

To record credit transactions in accounts

. Open an Account for each aspect of transaction.
. Debit Purchases Account with value of goods bought on credit.
. Credit Supplier's Account with value of goods bought on credit.
. Debit Customer's Account with value of goods sold on credit.

Note

When credit transactions are numerous they are entered in books referred to as Sales Day Books and Purchase Day Books and only the totals of these books are posted to the Sales Account and Purchases Account once a month. (See section on Day Books page 12).

Example

Record the following credit transaction in the books of A. Draper.
1 Bought goods on credit from J. Smith £100
2 Sold goods on credit from R. Brown £50
3 Bought goods from A. Fox on credit £70
4 Sold goods to G. Box on credit £80

Solution to Example on page 4
Credit Transactions recorded in account form

DR	J. Smith Account	CR
	Purchases (1) £100	

DR	R. Brown Account	CR
Sales (2) £50		

DR	A. Fox Account	CR
	Purchases (3) £70	

DR	G. Box Account	CR
Sales (4) £80		

DR	Purchases Account	CR
J. Smith (1) £100		
A. Fox (3) 70		

DR	Sales Account	CR
	R. Brown (2) £50	
	G. Box (4) 80	

Notes
1. J. Smith and A. Fox are referred to as *Creditors* of A. Draper since the latter owes money to them for goods purchased on credit.
2. R. Brown and G. Box are referred to as *Debtors* since they both owe money to A. Draper for goods he sold on credit to them.
3. The figures shown in brackets in each Account refer to the transactions in the example and are *not* folios but used to illustrate the double-entry aspect of each transaction.

Balancing Accounts

Main Features

. The difference between the sides of an account is referred to as a *'balance'*.
. If amounts are recorded on both sides of an account the smaller sum is subtracted from the larger and the difference is shown as the *'balance'*. Both sides of the account are totalled and the *'balance'* brought down to the other side of the account thus completing the double entry.

Trial Balance

Main Features

. A trial balance is a statement in which are listed debit and credit balances extracted from accounts.
. A trial balance is *not* part of the double entry system.
. The debit balances should equal the credit balances.
. It provides an arithmetical check on the accuracy of the postings to the ledger.

For details see pages 46 and 47

Simple Illustration of Balancing an Account

DR			Cash Account (as shown previously)			CR
Capital	(1)	£1,000	Purchases	(2)	£300	
Sales	(3)	200	Office desk	(4)	50	
			Balance	c/d	850	
		£1,200			£1,200	
Balance	b/d	£850				

Using the information appearing in the foregoing accounts the Trial Balance would appear thus:

Trial Balance

	DR	CR
Cash	£850	
Capital		£1,000
Sales		200
Purchases	300	
Office desk	50	
	£1,200 =	£1,200

This proves that a debit entry has been made for every credit entry.

Classification of Business Transactions

It is necessary to classify the various types of business transactions so that they can be grouped together under specific headings. This system of classifying transactions simplifies the preparation of the Final Accounts of the business.

Main Headings

Assets
These consist of things which a business owns which enable it to operate.
Examples: Buildings, land, plant, machinery, motor cars, stock of goods, amounts due by debtors, cash in hand and in bank.

Liabilities
These are debts which the business owes.
Examples: Bank overdraft, debts due to suppliers, loans.

Expenses
These are amounts spent by the business from which the benefit has been consumed during the accounting period.
Examples: Purchases of goods for resale, wages, salaries, rent, rates, electricity, telephone, printing and stationery, discount allowed, etc.

Income
These are amounts of sales and other income the business has received
Examples: Sales to customers, rent received, commission received, discount received, etc.

Capital
This represents the amount of money invested by the owner of the business
Example: Capital account of the owner of the business.

Capital and Revenue Expenditure

Purpose

It is essential to draw a distinction between capital and revenue expenditure if a true and correct profit or loss is to be calculated. In simple terms profit earned in a business is calculated by deducting total revenue expenditure from the gross sales income received. (Capital Expenditure is excluded from this calculation and is shown in the Balance Sheet under the Assets heading.)

Capital Expenditure

This is expenditure on the purchase of assets; in other words items of value which will remain in the business for a considerable time and will increase its earning power and its income. These items are classified under Assets.

Revenue Expenditure

This type of expenditure represents money spent by the business on immediately consumable items and all current expenses of carrying on the business. These items are classified under Expenses.

Examples

The following are examples of Capital and Revenue Expenditure:

Capital Expenditure	Revenue Expenditure
Land	Rent and rates
Buildings	Heat and light
Motor vehicles	Printing and stationery
Furniture and fittings	Wages and salaries
Machinery	Insurance
Patents and Trade Marks	Repairs

Divisions of the Ledger

Purpose   When there are many business transactions to be recorded and the number of accounts increases it becomes necessary to analyse these accounts and record them in separate ledgers.

Types of Accounts   Accounts may be divided into the following classifications:

Personal:
Accounts of persons, firms and companies relating to credit accounts of customers and suppliers.
Examples: Personal accounts of debtors and creditors of the business.
Real: accounts which are tangible in nature.
Examples: Buildings, plant, machinery, motor cars, office fittings etc.
Nominal: accounts recording items of income and expenditure.
Examples: Purchases, sales, wages, electricity, rent, rates etc.

Divisions of the Ledger   Accounts are written up in a book referred to as a Ledger. With the increase in the number of accounts in an expanding business it is necessary to split the Ledger into divisions which are:
Purchases Ledger: (or Creditors' Ledger)
This Ledger records the personal aspect of credit transactions for the supply of all goods and services.
Sales Ledger: (or Debtors' Ledger)
This Ledger records the personal aspect of credit transactions for the sale of all goods and services.
Impersonal Ledger: (or Nominal Ledger or General Ledger)
This Ledger records all real and nominal accounts.
Cash Ledger: (Cash Book including Cash Account and Bank Account)
This Ledger which is usually referred to as a Cash Book records business receipts and payments made by cheque or cash.

Books of Original Entry

Books of Original Entry	. Purchases Day Book.
	. Purchases Returns Book.
	. Sales Day Book.
	. Sales Returns Book.
	. Cash Book (although basically a ledger it is considered a book of original entry).
	. Petty Cash Book.
	. Journal.

Main Features
. One aspect of every transaction must be recorded in a Book of Original Entry.
. The basic information from the original business document (e.g. invoice, cheque etc.) is recorded in the books of original entry before being entered in the Ledger.
The entries in the ledger are made in all cases from the appropriate books of original entry.

Purchases Day Book

Purpose

The Purchases Day Book is used to record and analyse all purchases for goods and services supplied on credit.

Main Features

- A book of original entry.
- Details of credit transactions are taken from the purchase invoice.
- Provides total of purchases for period usually a month.
- Cash purchases are not recorded in purchases day book.
- Trade discount is shown as a deduction in the day book only.
- Can be used as method of analysing credit purchases.

Instructions

To Write up Purchases Day Book

Col 1 Date of transaction.

2 Creditor's name and details of transaction.

3 Creditor's ledger folio.

4 Amount of each item on invoice less any trade discount.

5 Extend invoice total.

Postings from Purchases Day Book to Ledger.

- Each credit purchase posted to credit side of creditor's account.
- Total credit purchases posted to debit side of purchases account.

Example

A. Draper has the following credit purchases in June.

June 5 From J. Brown —   4 coats @ *£10* each

7 From B. Green —   5 shirts @*£5* each

3 ties   @*£3* each

15 From W. Smith —   10 suits @*£30* each

Less trade discount $33^1/_3$%.

Enter the above transactions in the Purchases Day Book and post to the appropriate Ledger Accounts.

See page 126 for example of Purchase invoice.

Purchases Day Book Ruling (Solution to Example on page 12)

	Purchases Day Book				Folio PDB 1
Date **1**	Details **2**	Folio **3**	Amount **4**		Amount **5**
June 5	J. Brown — 4 coats @ £10 each	$\frac{PL}{B1}$			£40.00
7	B. Green — 5 shirts @ £5 each	$\frac{PL}{G1}$	£25.00		
	3 ties @ £3 each		9.00		34.00
15	W. Smith — 10 suits @ £30 each		300.00		
	Less: Trade discount $33\frac{1}{3}$ %	$\frac{PL}{S1}$	100.00		200.00
	Posted to Purchases Account	$\frac{IL}{P1}$			£274.00

Purchases Ledger

DR		J. Brown A/C		(B1)	CR
	June 5	Purchases	$\frac{PDB}{1}$	£40	

DR		B. Green A/C		(G1)	CR
	June 7	Purchases	$\frac{PDB}{1}$	£34	

DR		W. Smith A/C		(S1)	CR
	June 15	Purchases	$\frac{PDB}{1}$	£200	

Impersonal Ledger

DR		Purchases A/C		(P1)	CR
	June 30	Total from PDB	$\frac{PDB}{1}$	£274	

Purchases Day Book can be used as an Analysis Book — Alternative Presentation

Date	Details	Folio	Amount	Amount	Coats	Shirts and Ties	Suits
June 5	J. Brown — 4 coats @ £10 each	$\frac{PL}{B1}$		£40.00	£40.00		
7	B. Green — 5 shirts @ £5 each	$\frac{PL}{G1}$	£25.00				
	3 ties @ £3 each		9.00	34.00		£34.00	
15	W. Smith — 10 suits @ £30 each		£300.00				
	Less: Trade discount $33\frac{1}{3}$%	$\frac{PL}{S1}$	100.00	200.00			£200.00
				£274.00	£40.00	£34.00	£200.00

Sales Day Book

Purpose

The Sales Day Book is used to record and analyse all goods and services sold on credit.

Main Features

. A book of original entry.
. Details of credit sales are taken from sales invoices.
. Provides total of sales for period usually a month.
. Cash sales are not recorded in Sales Day Book.
. Trade discount is shown as a deduction in the Day Book only.
. Can be used as a method of analysing credit sales.

Instructions

To Write up Sales Day Book
Col 1 Date of transaction.
  2 Debtor's name and details of transaction.
  3 Debtor's ledger folio.
  4 Amount of each item on invoice less any trade discount.
  5 Extend invoice total.

Postings from Sales Day Book to Ledger
. Each credit sale posted to debit side of debtor's account.
. Total credit sales posted to credit side of sales account.

Example

A. Draper has the following credit sales in June.
June 8 To B. Black –   2 suits   @ £50 each
    15 To C. Blue –   3 ties   @ £ 2 each
                        1 overcoat @£30
    20 To D. Stewart –5 shirts   @ £6 each
                        Less trade discount 30%.

Enter the above transactions in the Sales Day Book and post to the appropriate Ledger Accounts.

See page 127 for example of Sales invoice.

Sales Day Book Ruling (Solution to Example on page 14)

Sales Day Book				Folio SDB 1
Date **1**	Details **2**	Folio **3**	Amount **4**	Amount **5**
June 8	B. Black 2 suits @ £50 each	$\frac{SL}{B1}$		£100.00
15	C. Blue 3 ties @ £2 each	$\frac{SL}{B2}$	£6.00	
	1 overcoat @ £30		30.00	36.00
20	D. Stewart 5 shirts @ £6 each		£30.00	
	Less: Trade discount 30%	$\frac{SL}{S1}$	9.00	21.00
	Posted to Sales Account	$\frac{IL}{S1}$		£157.00

Sales Ledger

DR   **B. Black A/C**   **(B1)**   **CR**

June 8	Sales	$\frac{SDB}{1}$	£100				

DR   **C. Blue A/C**   **(B2)**   **CR**

June 15	Sales	$\frac{SDB}{1}$	£36				

DR   **D. Stewart A/C**   **(S1)**   **CR**

June 20	Sales	$\frac{SDB}{1}$	£21				

Impersonal Ledger

DR   **Sales A/C**   **(S1)**   **CR**

				June 30	Total from SDB	$\frac{SDB}{1}$	£157

Sales Day Book — Can be used as an Analysis Book — Alternative Presentation

Date	Details	Folio	Amount	Amount	Suits	Shirts and Ties	Coats
June 8	B. Black 2 suits @ £50 each	$\frac{SL}{B1}$		£100.00	£100.00		
15	C. Blue 3 ties @ £2 each	$\frac{SL}{B2}$	£6.00			£6.00	
	1 overcoat @ £30		30.00	36.00			£30.00
20	D. Stewart 5 shirts @ £6 each	$\frac{SL}{S1}$	30.00				
	Less: Trade discount		9.00	21.00		21.00	
				£157.00	£100.00	£27.00	£30.00

Purchases Returns Book

Purpose   To record returns of goods bought on credit.

Main Features
- A book of original entry.
- Details of returns are taken from credit note.
- Provides total of purchases returns for period usually a month.
- Errors in pricing on purchase invoice are adjusted through this book.
- Subsidiary columns can be used to analyse returns.
- Trade discount is deducted from returns if applicable.

Instructions

To Write up Purchases Returns Book
Col 1 Date of transaction.
    2 Creditor's name and details of returns.
    3 Creditor's ledger folio.
    4 Amount of each item on credit note.
    5 Extend credit note total.

Postings from Purchases Returns Book to Ledger
- Each purchases return posted to debit side of creditor's account.
- Total purchases returns posted to credit side of Purchases Returns Account.

Example

A. Draper has the following returns to suppliers.
June 7 To J. Brown — 1 coat damaged @ *£10*
    18 To W. Smith — 1 suit faulty   @ *£30*
                       Less trade discount $33^1/3\%$.

Enter the above transactions in the Purchases Returns Book and post to the appropriate Ledger Accounts.

See page 128 for example of credit note.

Purchases Returns Book Ruling (Solution to Example on page 16)

Purchases Returns Book				Folio PRB 1
Date 1	Details 2	Folio 3	Amount 4	Amount 5
June 7 18	J. Brown — Return of 1 coat damaged @ £10 W. Smith — Return of 1 suit faulty @ £30 *Less:* Trade discount $33\frac{1}{3}$% Posted to Purchases Returns A/C	$\frac{PL}{B1}$ $\frac{PL}{S1}$ $\frac{IL}{P2}$	 £30.00 10.00	£10.00 20.00 £30.00

Purchases Ledger

DR				J. Brown A/C		(B1)		CR
June 7	Returns	$\frac{PRB}{1}$	£10					

DR				W. Smith A/C		(S1)		CR
June 18	Returns	$\frac{PRB}{1}$	£20					

Impersonal Ledger

DR				Purchases Returns A/C		(P2)		CR
				June 30	Total from PRB	$\frac{PRB}{1}$	£30	

Note: The Purchases Returns Book can be ruled in analysed form in the same manner as the Purchases Day Book.

17

Sales Returns Book

Purpose	To record returns of goods sold on credit.
Main Features	. A book of original entry.
	. Details of returns are taken from credit note.
	. Provides total of sales returns for period usually a month.
	. Errors in pricing on sales invoice are adjusted through this book.
	. Subsidiary columns can be used to analyse returns.
	. Trade discount is deducted from returns if applicable.

Instructions

To Write up Sales Returns Book
Col 1 Date of transaction.
      2 Debtor's name and details of returns.
      3 Debtor's ledger folio.
      4 Amount of each item on credit note.
      5 Extend credit note total.

Postings from Sales Returns Book to Ledger
. Each sales returns posted to credit side of debtor's account.
. Total sales returns posted to debit side of sales returns account.

Example

A. Draper has the following returns from customers.
June 10 From B. Black   — 1 tie   @ £2 wrong colour
      25 From D. Stewart — 1 shirt @ £6 damaged
                                      Less trade discount 30%

Enter the above transactions in the Sales Returns Book and post to the appropriate Ledger Accounts.

See page 129 for example of credit note.

Sales Returns Book Ruling (Solution to Example on page 18)

	Sales Returns Book			Folio SRB1	
Date 1	Details 2	Folio 3	Amount 4	Amount 5	
June 10	B. Black 1 tie @ £2 returned wrong colour	SL B1		£2.00	
25	D. Stewart 1 shirt @ £6 returned damaged *Less:* Trade discount 30%	SL B2	£6.00 1.80	4.20	
	Posted to Sales Returns Account	IL S2		£6.20	

Sales Ledger

DR					B. Black A/C			(B1)	CR
					June 10	Returns	SRB 1	£2.00	

DR					D. Stewart A/C			(B2)	CR
					June 25	Returns	SRB 1	£4.20	

Impersonal Ledger

DR			Sales Returns A/C			(S2)	CR
June 30	Total from SRB	SRB 1	£6.20				

Note: The Sales Returns Book can be ruled in analysed form in the same manner as the Sales Day Book.

Cash Book (Two Column)

Purpose   To record receipts and payments made in cash or by cheque.

Main Features
- Book of original entry.
- Contains two accounts — bank account and cash account.
- Debit side records receipts of cash and cheques.
- Credit side records payments by cash and cheques.

Instructions   *To Write up Two Column Cash Book*

Debit Side	Credit Side
Col 1 Date of transaction	Col 1 Date of transaction
2 Narrative of transaction	2 Narrative of transaction
3 Ledger account folio	3 Ledger account folio
4 Amount received in cash	4 Amount paid in cash
5 Amount received by cheque	5 Amount paid by cheque

Postings from Cash Book to Ledger

Cash Book	Ledger
Dr. Cash/cheque from debtors.	Cr. Debtors' accounts — — Sales Ledger.
Dr. Receipts from other sources.	Cr. Nominal or real accounts — Impersonal Ledger.
Cr. Cash/cheque to creditors.	Dr. Creditors' accounts — Purchase Ledger.
Cr. Payments for expenses.	Dr. Nominal or real accounts — Impersonal Ledger.

Cash from Bank (Contra)	Cash to Bank (Contra)
Dr. Cash book — Cash column.	Dr. Cash book — Bank column.
Cr. Cash book — Bank column.	Cr. Cash book — Cash column.

Example   A. Draper had the following cash book transactions in June.

June 1 The cash balance amounted to £55 and the cash at bank was £75.
   8 Received from J. Smith (debtor) £50 by cheque.
   12 Received commission in cash £10.
   15 Transferred £60 from bank to cash.
   17 Paid R. Brown (creditor) £80 by cheque.
   20 Paid wages in cash £90.

Transactions Recorded in Separate Bank and Cash Accounts
(Solution to Example on page 20)

DR   **Cash Account**   **CR**

June 1	Balance	b/d	£55	June 20	Wages	IL/W1	£90
12	Commission	IL/C1	10	30	Balance	c/d	35
15	Bank	(c)	60				
			£125				£125
July 1	Balance	b/d	£35				

DR   **Bank Account**   **CR**

June 1	Balance	b/d	£75	June 15	Cash	(c)	£60
8	J. Smith	SL/S1	50	17	R. Brown	PL/B1	80
30	Balance	c/d	15				
			£140				£140
				July 1	Balance	b/d	£15

Transactions Recorded in Two Column Cash Book

DR   **Cash Book**   **(CB1)**   **CR**

Date 1	Details 2	Folio 3	Cash 4	Bank 5	Date 1	Details 2	Folio 3	Cash 4	Bank 5
June 1	Balance	b/d	£55	£75	June 15	Cash	(c)		£60
8	J. Smith	SL/S1		50	17	R. Brown	PL/B1		80
12	Commission	IL/C1	10		20	Wages	IL/W1	£90	
15	Bank	(c)	60						
30	Balance	c/d		15	30	Balance	c/d	35	
			£125	£140				£125	£140
July 1	Balance	b/d	£35		July 1	Balance	b/d		£15

Sales Ledger   **Purchases Ledger**

DR   J. Smith A/C   **(S1) CR**   **DR**   R. Brown A/C   **(B1) CR**

	June 8	Bank	CB/1	£50	June 17	Bank	CB/1	£80	

Impersonal Ledger   **Impersonal Ledger**

DR   Commission A/C   **(C1) CR**   **DR**   Wages Account   **(W1) CR**

	June 12	Cash	CB/1	£10	June 20	Cash	CB/1	£90	

Note: Opening balances for cash in hand and cash at bank are recorded before entering transactions.

Closing balances are entered in 'old' period and brought down to 'new' period. In this example the Bank Account is overdrawn to the extent of £15.

See page 130 for example of cheque and paying-in slip.

Cash Book (Three Column)

Purpose   To record receipts and payments made in cash or by cheque.

Main Features
. Book of Original Entry.
. Contains two accounts — Bank Account and Cash Account.
. Debit side records receipts of cash and cheques.
. Credit side records payments by cash and cheques.
. Two additional columns are included.
. Debit side — discount allowed.
. Credit side — discount received.
. Discount columns do *not* form part of the double entry system.

Instructions   *To Write up Three-Column Cash Book*

Debit side	Credit side
Col 1 Date of transaction	Col 1 Date of transaction
2 Narrative of transaction	2 Narrative of transaction
3 Ledger account folio	3 Ledger account folio
4 Discount allowed	4 Discount received
5 Amount received in cash	5 Amount paid in cash
6 Amount received by cheque	6 Amount paid by cheque

Postings from Cash Book to Ledger
See Cash Book two Column page 20

Contra Accounts
See Cash Book two Column page 20

Example   A. Draper has the following cash book transactions in June.
June 1   Cash balance amounted to £55 and the cash at Bank was £75.
    8   Received from J. Smith (debtor) £50 by cheque, discount allowed was £2.
  12   Received commission in cash £10.
  15   Transferred £60 from bank to cash.
  17   Paid R. Brown (creditor) £80 by cheque, discount received was £4.
  20   Paid wages in cash £90.

Transactions Recorded in Three Column Cash Book
(Solution to Example on page 22)

DR					Cash Book			(CB1)		CR

Date	Details	Folio	Discount allowed	Cash	Bank	Date	Details	Folio	Discount received	Cash	Bank
1	2	3	4	5	6	1	2	3	4	5	6
June 1	Balances	b/d		£55	£75	June 15	Cash	(c)			£60
8	J. Smith	$\frac{SL}{S1}$	£2		50	17	R. Brown	$\frac{PL}{B1}$	£4		80
12	Commission	$\frac{IL}{C1}$		10		20	Wages	$\frac{IL}{W1}$		£90	
15	Bank	(c)		60		30	Balance	c/d		35	
30	Balance	c/d			15						
			£2	£125	£140				£4	£125	£140
July 1	Balance	b/d	$\frac{IL}{D2}$	£35		July 1	Balance	b/d	$\frac{IL}{D1}$		£15

Sales Ledger

DR		J. Smith A/C		(S1) CR
	June 8	Bank	$\frac{CB}{1}$	£50
		Discount	$\frac{CB}{1}$	2

Purchases Ledger

DR		R. Brown A/C		(B1) CR
	June 7	Bank	$\frac{CB}{1}$	£80
		Discount	$\frac{CB}{1}$	4

Impersonal Ledger

DR		Commission A/C		(S1) CR
	June 12	Cash	$\frac{CB}{1}$	£10

DR		Wages A/C		(W1) CR
	June 20	Cash	$\frac{CB}{1}$	£90

DR	Discount Allowed A/C		(D2) CR
June 30	Total from Cash Book	$\frac{CB}{1}$ £2	

DR	Discount Received A/C		(DI) CR
	June 30	Total from Cash Book	$\frac{CB}{1}$ £4

Method of Balancing Three Column Cash Book

Instructions
Balancing Cash Columns
Step 1 Leave space for *'balance'* amount in cash column on side which has smaller total.
   2 Add cash column with larger total.
   3 Insert total as calculated in Step 2 on the opposite side of the cash column.
   4 Add the column with the smaller total.
   5 Subtract the smaller from the greater total and insert the *'balance'* in the space left in Step 1.
   6 Bring down *'balance'* to the new period on the opposite side of the column below the total.

To Balance Bank Columns
Follow the same steps as for cash columns.

Points to Note
Balancing Cash and Bank Columns
. If total of the credit bank column is greater than the debit bank column then the 'balance' represents an overdraft as in the example.
. The cash balance must always be at debit.
. Discount columns are memoranda columns and are totalled but not balanced.
. Total of discount allowed is posted to debit of discount allowed account.
. Total of discount received is posted to credit of discount received account.

Method of Balancing Three Column Cash Book

Cash Book

DR

Date	Details	Folio	Discount allowed	Cash	Bank
June 1	Balances	b/d		£55	£75
8	J. Smith	SL/S1	£2		50
12	Commission	IL/C1		10	
15	Bank	(c)		60	
30	Balance	b/d			15
			£2	£125	£140
July 1	Balance	b/d		£35	

CR

Date	Details	Folio	Discount received	Cash	Bank
June 15	Cash	(c)			£60
17	R. Brown	PL/B1	£4		80
20	Wages	IL/W1		£90	
30	Balance	c/d		£35	
			£4	£125	£140
July 1	Balance	b/d		£15	

Petty Cash Book
(Normal System)

Purpose

As a subsidiary cash book it is used to record small cash transactions.

Main Features

. Book of Original Entry.
. Details of payments are taken from petty cash vouchers.
. Debit side records cash from main cash book.
. Credit side records cash payments.
. Can be analysed to provide totals of cash payments. for period under appropriate headings.

Instructions

To Write up Petty Cash Book — Normal System
Col. 1 Amount of cash received from Principal Cashier.
    2 Main Cash Book folio.
    3 Date of transactions.
    4 Details of transactions.
    5 Petty cash voucher reference number.
    6 Enter expenses amount
    7, 8 & 9 Analysis of expenditure under appropriate headings.

Postings from Cash Book	*Postings to Impersonal Ledger*
. Debit Petty Cash Book with cash transferred from Main Cash Book.	. Debit appropriate accounts in Impersonal Ledger with cash expenditure.
. Credit Main Cash Book.	. Credit Petty Cash Book.

To Balance Petty Cash Book Written up on Normal System
Step 1 Total Credit side and enter amount of expenditure.
    2 Enter difference between total in step 1 and the receipts column of the Petty Cash Book.
    3 Bring down balance calculated in step 2 to 'new' period.
    4 Total analysis column.

Example

A.Draper has the following petty cash transactions in June. June 1 Cash from Main Cash Book £30. June 2 Postages £2. June 5 Envelopes £3. June 19 Notepaper £5. June 25 Office tea £1.

Example of Petty Cash Book — 'Normal' System

			Petty Cash Book				PCB1	
Receipts 1	Folio 2	Date 3	Details 4	Voucher No. 5	Total 6	Postages 7	Stationery 8	Sundries 9
£30	CB̲ 1	June 1	Cash					
		2	Postages	1	£2	£2		
		5	Envelopes	2	3		£3	
		19	Notepaper	3	5		5	
		25	Office tea	4	1			£1
					❶£11	❹ £2	❹ £8	❹ £1
		30	Balance	c/d	19	I̲L̲	I̲L̲	I̲L̲
£3̲0̲					❷£̲3̲0̲	P3	S3	S4
£19❸	b/d	July 1	Balance				❹	

DR			Cash Book (Cash Column)		CBI	CR
			June 1	Petty cash	PCB̲ 1	£30

Impersonal Ledger

DR			Postages A/C			(P3)		CR
June 30	Total from PCB	PCB̲ 1	£2					

DR			Stationery A/C			(S3)		CR
June 30	Total from PCB	PCB̲ 1	£8					

DR			Sundries A/C			(S4)		CR
June 30	Total from PCB	PCB̲ 1	£1					

See page 130 for example of petty cash voucher.

Petty Cash Book (Imprest System)

Purpose

As a subsidiary cash book it is used to record small cash transactions.

Main Features

. Book of Original Entry.
. Details of payments are taken from petty cash vouchers.
. A fixed sum of cash is held by the Petty Cashier.
. From this 'fixed sum' or 'imprest' all petty cash payments are made and recorded on Credit side.
. Can be analysed to provide totals of cash payments for period under appropriate headings.
. At agreed intervals the exact amount of cash paid out (total expenses paid) is handed over by the Principal Cashier to the Petty Cashier to restore the petty cash in hand to the original 'imprest amount'.

Instructions

To Write up Petty Cash Book under Imprest System.
Col. 1 Enter cash received from Principal Cashier.
  2 Main Cash Book folio.
  3 Date of transactions.
  4 Detail of transactions.
  5 Petty cash voucher reference number.
  6 Enter expenses amount.
  7, 8 & 9 Analysis of expenditure under appropriate headings.

Postings from Cash Book
. Debit Petty Cash Book with cash transferred from Main Cash Book.
. Credit Main Cash Book.

Postings to Impersonal Ledger
. Debit appropriate accounts in Impersonal Ledger with cash expenditure.
. Credit Petty Cash Book.

To Balance Petty Cash Book Written up on 'Imprest' System
Step 1 Enter 'imprest' amount as a balance on payments side
  2 Total Credit side of Petty Cash Book excluding 'imprest' amount.
  3 Enter amount calculated in Step 2 as cash reimbursement on receipts side.
  4 Bring down 'imprest' amount as balance to 'new' period.
  5 Total analysis columns.

Example

A. Draper has the following petty cash transactions in June.
June 1 Imprest amount from Main Cash Book £30. June 2 Postages £2. June 5 Envelopes £3. June 19 Notepaper £5. June 25 Office tea £1.

Example of Petty Cash Book: 'Imprest' System Assuming 'Imprest' amount £30

Petty Cash Book   PCB1

Receipts 1	Folio 2	Date 3	Details 4	Voucher No. 5	Total 6	Postages 7	Stationery 8	Sundries 9
£30	CB 1	June 1	Cash					
		2	Postages	1	£2	£2		
		5	Envelopes	2	3		£3	
		19	Notepaper	3	5		5	
		25	Office tea	4	1			£1
					£11	£2	£8	£1
£11	CB 1	30	Cash — Reimbursement	c/d		IL	IL	IL
			Balance		£30	P3	S3	S4
£41					£41	Posted to Impersonal Ledger as Normal System.		
£30	b/d	July 1	Balance					

Journal

Purpose

To record any transaction which cannot first be entered in a book of original entry before being posted to the Ledger. In other words any transaction where both aspects are only entered in ledger accounts.

Basic Principle of Double Entry Accounting

Any entry in a ledger account must first of all be recorded in a book of original entry. Some transactions which neither involve cash or credit aspects are not entered in the Cash Book or day books must first of all be entered in the Journal.

Main Features

. Book of original entry.
. Records the debit and credit entries of each transaction for posting to the Ledger Accounts.
. Includes a narrative explaining the transaction.

Instructions

To Write up the Journal
Col 1 Enter date of transaction.
 2 Enter account to be debited. Show 'DR' before folio column.
   Enter account to be credited below and slightly to the right of debit entry prefixed by word 'To'.
 3 Enter ledger folios of 'DR' and 'CR' entries.
 4 Enter amount of debit entry.
 5 Enter amount of credit entry.

Show narrative explaining nature of transaction.

Postings to the Ledger
The entries are posted to the ledger in the normal way.

Examples

1 *Purchase of Fixed Asset on Credit*
This transaction would require to be entered through the Journal if no entry was made in the Purchases Day Book.

On June 1 A. Draper purchased on credit from Engineers Ltd. fixtures costing *£100.*

2 *Opening Entries*
The opening entries to open the books of a business are required to be recorded through the Journal.

A. Draper started business on January 1 with *£1,000* capital represented by the following assets: motor car *£500,* fittings *£200* and stock of goods *£300.*

Example of Journal Ruling

On Jan 1 an item of plant costing £100 has been posted to the repairs account in error.

Journal			Folio (J.1)	
Date 1	Details 2	Folio 3	Amount 4	Amount 5
Jan 1	Plant DR	IL/P5	£100	
	To Repairs	IL/R3		£100
	Being plant posted to repairs account in error now adjusted			

Purchase of Fixed Asset on Credit (Solution to Example 1 on page 30)

Journal			Folio (J.1)	
June 1	Fixtures DR	IL/F2	£100	
	To Engineers Ltd	PL/E3		£100
	Being fixtures purchased on credit			

DR	Fixtures Account	F2	CR	DR	Engineers Ltd. A/C	E3	CR
June 1	Engineers Ltd.	J1	£100		June 1	Fixtures	J1	£100

Opening Entries (Solution to Example 2 on page 30)

Journal			Folio (J.1)	
Jan 1	Motor car DR	IL/M2	£500	
	Fittings	IL/F4	200	
	Stock	IL/S4	300	
	To Capital	IL/C1		£1,000
	Being assets introduced by A. Draper as his capital at start of business			

This is referred to as a compound Journal Entry as there is more than one account to debit. However both sides must still agree in total.

DR	Motor Car A/C	M2	CR	DR	Fittings Account	F4	CR
Jan 1	Capital	J1	£500		Jan 1	Capital	J1	£200

DR	Stock Account	S4	CR	DR	Capital Account	C1	CR
Jan 1	Capital	J1	£300		Jan 1	Sundries	J1	£1,000

Note: The narrative 'sundries' is used in the Capital Account since it includes several items.

Journal (cont.)

Examples (cont'd.)   3 *Closing Entries*

At the close of each financial period the amounts in respect of revenue expenditure and income are transferred to the Trading and Profit and Loss Accounts to enable a profit or loss on trading to be calculated.

On 31 December A. Draper has the following balances on the undernoted accounts which have to be closed off to the Trading and Profit and Loss Accounts: Purchases Account, 'DR' *£3,000*, Sales Account 'CR' *£4,000* and Salaries Account 'DR' *£500*.

Closing Entries (Solution to Example 3 on page 32)

Journal				Folio (J.1)	
Dec 31	Trading Account DR To Purchases Being transfer of purchases for period	IL/T2 IL/P1	£3,000		£3,000
	Sales DR To Trading Account Being transfer of sales for period	IL/S1 IL/T2	£4,000		£4,000
	Trading Account DR To Profit and Loss A/c. Being transfer of gross profit for period	IL/T2 IL/P6	£1,000		£1,000
	Profit and Loss Account DR To Salaries Being transfer of salaries for period	IL/P6 IL/S4	£500		£500

DR			Purchases Account			(P 1)	CR
Dec 31	Balance	b/d	£3,000	Dec. 31	Trading	J1	£3,000

DR			Sales Account			(S1)	CR
Dec. 31	Trading	J1	£4,000	Dec. 31	Balance	b/d	£4,000

DR			Salaries Account			(S4)	CR
Dec. 31	Balance	b/d	£500	Dec. 31	Profit and Loss	J1	£500

DR			Trading Account			(T2)	CR
Dec. 31	Purchases Profit and Loss	J1 J1	£3,000 1,000 __£4,000__	Dec. 31	Sales	J1	£4,000 __£4,000__

DR			Profit and Loss Account			(P6)	CR
Dec. 31	Salaries	J1	£500	Dec. 31	Trading	J1	£1,000

Purchases Ledger

The Purchases Ledger is used to record details of the personal aspects of all transactions affecting purchases of goods or services on credit.

Instructions

To Write up Purchases Ledger
Enter name of Creditor at top of account with ledger folio reference.

Debit Side	Credit Side
Col 1 Date of transaction	Col 1 Date of transaction
2 Narrative of Book of Original Entry	2 Narrative of Book of Original Entry
3 Folio of Book of Original Entry	3 Folio of Book of Original Entry
4 Amount of transaction	4 Amount of transaction

Postings to Purchases Ledger from Books of Original Entry

Debit Side

Narrative in Ledger	Source of Transaction
Returns	Purchases Returns Book
Cash	Cash Book
Bank	Cash Book
Discount received	Cash Book

Credit Side

Narrative in Ledger	Source of Transaction
Purchases	Purchases Day Book

Example

A. Draper had the following transactions in June:
June 15 Bought on credit from W. Smith goods *£300*
18 Returned goods damaged to W. Smith *£100.*
21 Paid cheque in settlement of W. Smith's account less 5% discount *£190.*

Solution to Example on page 34

Purchases Ledger

DR					W. Smith Account	Folio (S.1)		CR
1	**2**	**3**	**4**	**1**	**2**	**3**	**4**	
June 18	Returns	PRB 1	£100	June 15	Purchases	PDB 1	£300	
21	Bank	CB 1	190					
	Discount received	CB 1	10					
			£300				£300	

The information recorded in the above Ledger Account would be posted from the following books of Original Entry.

Purchases Day Book			Folio (PDB.1)	
Date	Details	Folio	Amount	Amount
June 15	W. Smith — Goods	PL S1		£300

Cash Book				Folio (CB.1)	CR
Date	Details	Folio	Discount received	Cash	Bank
June 21	W. Smith	PL S1	£10		£190

Purchases Returns Book			Folio (PRB.1)	
Date	Details	Folio	Amount	Amount
June 18	W. Smith — Damaged goods	PL S1		£100

Sales Ledger

Purpose   The Sales Ledger is used to record details of the personal aspects of all Sales of goods or services on credit.

Instructions   *To Write up Sales Ledger*
        Enter name of debtor at top of account with ledger folio reference.

Debit Side	Credit Side
Col 1 Enter date of transaction	Col 1 Enter date of transaction
2 Enter narrative from book of original entry	2 Enter narrative from book of original entry
3 Enter folio of book of original entry	3 Enter folio of book of original entry
4 Enter amount of transaction	4 Enter amount of transaction

Postings to Sales Ledger from Books of Original Entry

Debit Side

Narrative in Ledger	Source of Transaction
Sales	Sales Day Book

Credit Side

Narrative in Ledger	Source of Transaction
Returns	Sales Returns Book
Cash	Cash Book
Bank	Cash Book
Discount Allowed	Cash Book
Bad Debts	Journal

Example   A. Draper had the following transactions in June:
June 8 Sold on credit goods to B. Black £100.
        20 B. Black returns goods faulty £20.
        27 Received cheque from B. Black for amount due less 5% discount £76.

Sales Ledger (Solution to Example on page 36)

DR				B. Black Account		Folio B.1	CR
1	**2**	**3**	**4**	**1**	**2**	**3**	**4**
June 8	Sales	$\frac{SDB}{1}$	£100	June 20	Returns	$\frac{SRB}{1}$	£20
				27	Bank	$\frac{CB}{1}$	76
					Discount allowed	$\frac{CB}{1}$	4
			£100				£100

The information recorded in the above Ledger Account would be posted from the following books of Original Entry.

	Sales Day Book		Folio SDB1	
Date	Details	Folio	Amount	Amount
June 8	B. Black — Goods	$\frac{SL}{B1}$		£100

Debit Side		Cash Book		Folio CB1	
Date	Details	Folio	Discount allowed	Cash	Bank
June 27	B. Black	$\frac{SL}{B1}$	£4		£76

	Sales Returns Book		Folio SRB1	
Date	Details	Folio	Amount	Amount
June 20	B. Black — Faulty Goods	$\frac{SL}{B1}$		£20

Purchases Ledger Control Account

Purpose: The Purchases Ledger Control Account is used as a simple and effective technique to control the arithmetical accuracy of the postings from the books of original entry to the Ledger and is a useful method of obtaining total Creditors' balances without extracting a complete list of Creditors from the Ledger.

Instructions: *To write up a Purchases Ledger Control Account*

Debit Side		Credit Side	
Item	*Source*	*Item*	*Source*
Discount Received	❶ Cash Book	Balances	❺ Total of Opening Balances on Purchases Ledger
Cash Paid Returns	❷ Cash Book ❸ Purchases Returns Book	Purchases	❻ Total from Purchases Day Book
Balances	❹ Total of Purchase Ledger closing balances	Cash Refund Received from Creditor	❼ Cash Book

. Items are Recorded *in total* on the same side of the Control Account as they would appear in the Personal Accounts in the Ledger.

. The total balances shown in the Control Account must agree with the total of the individual balances in the Creditors' Ledger.

Example   Record the following transactions in the Books of A. Draper and thereafter prepare a Purchases Ledger Control Account.
The opening balances in the Creditors' Accounts are:
JT £200 (CR): LB £95 (CR) and WG £5 (DR)
The transactions for the month were:
Goods bought on credit from JT £50 and LB £25
Cash payments were made to JT £90 (Cash Discount £5) and LB £15.
A cash refund was received from WG £5
Goods were returned to LB valued £9.

Solution to Example on page 38

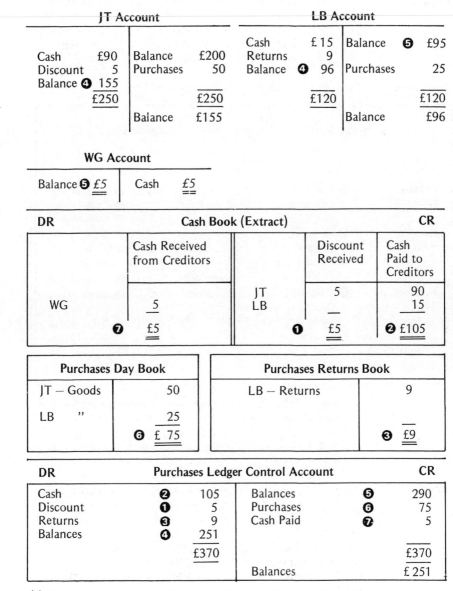

JT Account			
Cash	£90	Balance	£200
Discount	5	Purchases	50
Balance ❹	155		
	£250		£250
		Balance	£155

LB Account			
Cash	£15	Balance ❺	£95
Returns	9	Purchases	25
Balance ❹	96		
	£120		£120
		Balance	£96

WG Account			
Balance ❺ £5		Cash	£5

DR   **Cash Book (Extract)**   **CR**

	Cash Received from Creditors		Discount Received	Cash Paid to Creditors
WG	5	JT	5	90
		LB	—	15
❼	£5	❶	£5	❷ £105

Purchases Day Book	
JT – Goods	50
LB ,,	25
❻	£ 75

Purchases Returns Book	
LB – Returns	9
❸	£9

DR   **Purchases Ledger Control Account**   **CR**

Cash	❷	105	Balances	❺	290
Discount	❶	5	Purchases	❻	75
Returns	❸	9	Cash Paid	❼	5
Balances	❹	251			
		£370			£370
			Balances		£251

Notes: (a) Special columns would be required in Cash Book as shown above.
(b) If an item does not appear in the Personal Accounts in the Ledger it cannot be shown in the Purchase Ledger Control Account e.g. Cash Purchases.

Sales Ledger Control Account

Purpose   The Sales Ledger Control Account is used as a simple and effective technique to control the arithmetical accuracy of the postings from the books of original entry to the Ledger and is a useful method of obtaining total Debtors' Balances without extracting a complete list of Debtors from the Ledger.

Instructions   *To write up a Sales Ledger Control Account*

Debit Side		Credit Side	
Item	*Source*	*Item*	*Source*
Balance	❶ Total of Opening Balances on Sales Ledger	Discount Allowed Cash Paid Returns	❺ Cash Book ❻ Cash Book ❼ Sales Returns Book
Sales	❷ Total from Sales Day Book	Bad Debts	❽ Journal
Cash Refund Paid to Debtor	❸ Cash Book	Balances	❾ Total of Closing Balances on Sales Ledger
Dishonoured Cheque from Debtor	❹ Cash Book		

. Items are recorded *in total* on the same side of the Control Account as they would appear in the Personal Accounts in the Ledger.
. The total balances shown in the Control Account must agree with the total of the individual balances in the Debtors' Ledger.

Example   Record the following transactions in the Books of A. Draper and thereafter prepare a Sales Ledger Control Account. The opening balances in Debtors' Accounts are:

AB £500 (DR); CD £300 (DR) and EF £50 (CR)
The transactions for the month were:
Goods sold on credit to AB £200 and CD £100
Cash received from AB £400 (Cash Discount £10) and CD £300
A cash refund was paid to EF £50
Goods returned by AB amounted to £30.

Solution to Example on page 40

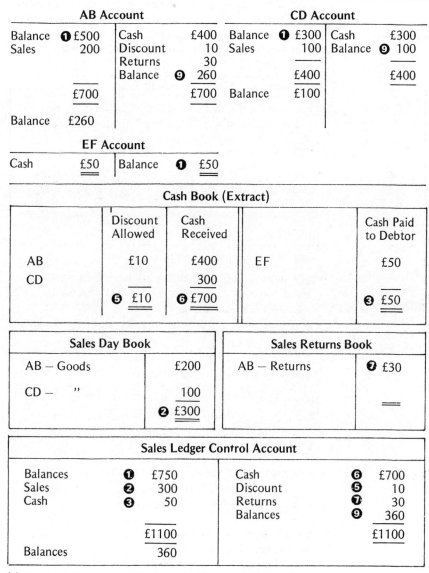

	AB Account			
Balance ❶ £500	Cash	£400
Sales 200	Discount	10
	Returns	30
	Balance ❾ 260
£700		£700
Balance £260	

	CD Account		
Balance ❶ £300	Cash	£300
Sales 100	Balance ❾ 100
£400		£400
Balance £100	

EF Account

Cash £50	Balance ❶ £50

Cash Book (Extract)

	Discount Allowed	Cash Received			Cash Paid to Debtor
AB	£10	£400	EF		£50
CD		300			
	❺ £10	❻ £700			❸ £50

Sales Day Book

AB – Goods	£200
CD – "	100
	❷ £300

Sales Returns Book

AB – Returns	❼ £30

Sales Ledger Control Account

Balances	❶	£750	Cash	❻	£700
Sales	❷	300	Discount	❺	10
Cash	❸	50	Returns	❼	30
			Balances	❾	360
		£1100			£1100
Balances		360			

Notes: (a) Special columns would be required in the Cash Book as shown above.
(b) If an item does not appear in the Personal Accounts in the Ledger it cannot be shown in the Sales Ledger Control Account e.g. Cash Sales.

Impersonal Ledger

Purpose

The Impersonal Ledger is used to record those accounts which are not included in the Sales or Purchases Ledger.

Instructions

To Write up Impersonal Ledger
Enter account heading with Ledger Folio reference at top of account.

Debit Side	Credit Side
Col 1 Date of transaction	Col 1 Date of transaction
2 Narrative of book of original entry	2 Narrative of book of original entry
3 Folio of book of original entry	3 Folio of book of original entry
4 Amount of transaction	4 Amount of transaction

Postings to Impersonal Ledger from Books of Original Entry

Debit Side

Type of items appearing on this side

Revenue expenditure — see Trial Balance list page 47
Purchase of assets — see Trial Balance list page 47
Personal drawings of owner
Reduction of liabilities — e.g. repayment of loan to business

Credit Side

Type of items appearing on this side

Revenue income — see Trial Balance list page 47
Liabilities — see Trial Balance list page 47
Capital of owner
Sale of assets e.g. proceeds of sale of car

Example

A. Draper had the following transactions in June:
June 8 Paid rent *£100* by cheque
     17 Received commission in cash *£20*
     25 Paid wages in cash *£200.*

Impersonal Ledger (Solution to Example on page 42)

DR				Rent Account	Folio (R.2)		CR
1	**2**	**3**	**4**	**1**	**2**	**3**	**4**
June 8	Bank	CB/1	£100				

DR				Commission Account		Folio (C.6)		CR
				June 17	Cash	CB/1	£20

DR				Wages Account	Folio (W.1)		CR
June 25	Cash	CB/1	£200				

DR						Cash Book		Folio (CB.1)		CR
Date	Details	Folio	Discount Allowed	Cash	Bank	Date	Details	Folio	Discount Received	Cash	Bank
June 17	Commission	IL/C6		£20		June 8	Rent	IL/R2			£100
						25	Wages	IL/W1		£200	

Balancing Ledger Accounts

Introduction

This method of balancing Ledger Accounts applies to the following:

Purchases Ledger
Sales Ledger
Impersonal Ledger.

Instructions

Step 1   Leave space for *'balance'* amount on side which has smaller total.
  2   Add the side with the larger total.
  3   Insert total as calculated in Step 2 on the opposite side of the account.
  4   Add the side with the smaller total.
  5   Subtract the smaller from the greater total and insert the *'balance'* in the space left in Step 1.
  6   Bring down *'balance'* to new period on the opposite side of the account below the total.

Points to Note

.   The total amounts must be entered on the same horizontal line.
.   The double entry principle is observed by showing the *'balance'* on both sides of the account — one above the total the other below.

Account with Balance at Debit
Sales Ledger

DR   A. Smith Account   CR

June 1	Sales	$\frac{SDB}{1}$	£500 ❷	June 30	Bank	$\frac{CB}{1}$	£200
					Discount allowed	$\frac{CB}{1}$	❹ 10
					Returns	$\frac{SRB}{1}$	30
					Balance	c/d	❶❺ 260
			£500		❻		❸ £500
July 1	Balance	b/d	£260				

Account with Balance at Credit
Purchases Ledger

DR   J. Brown Account   CR

June 30	Bank	$\frac{CB}{1}$	£150	June 1	Purchases	$\frac{PDB}{1}$	£250 ❷
	Discount received	$\frac{CB}{1}$	❹ 10				
	Returns	$\frac{PRB}{1}$	20				
	Balance	c/d	❶❺ 70				
			❸ £250		❻		£250
				July 1	Balance	b/d	£70

Account with Opening Balance
Impersonal Ledger

DR   Capital Account   CR

June 30	Balance	c/d	£1500	June 1	Balance	b/d	£1000
				15	Bank	$\frac{CB}{1}$	500
			£1500				£1500
				July 1	Balance	b/d	£1500

Trial Balance

Purpose

Trial Balance is a statement in which are listed debit and credit balances extracted from the ledgers.

Points to Note

. Trial Balance does *not* form part of the double-entry system.
. Total of debit balances equals total of credit balances.
. If Trial Balance is in agreement then it proves that the double entry principle has been correctly applied and that additions and balances are arithmetically correct, although there may be errors not disclosed by Trial Balance.

Instructions

To Write up Trial Balance
Enter debit balances from ledger accounts under 'DR' column.
Enter credit balances from ledger accounts under 'CR' column.

Errors in Trial Balance

Disclosed by Trial Balance
. Errors in additions of Trial Balance and Ledger Accounts.
. Balance entered on wrong side of Trial Balance.
. Balance missed out.
. Error in calculation of balance.
. Item incorrectly posted from book of original entry.
. Errors in additions in books of original entry.
. Incorrect amount recorded through bad writing or carelessness.

Not Disclosed by Trial Balance
. Errors of omission — where the original transaction is not entered in books.
. Errors of original entry — where the original entry is incorrectly recorded.
. Errors of principle — where a transaction has been treated incorrectly by being posted to the wrong class of account.
. Compensating errors — where errors occur on one side of the ledger but are compensated by equalizing errors on the other side.
. Errors of commission — where a transaction has been entered in an incorrect account of a similar type.

Trial Balance Checklist

Debit Balances		Credit Balances
Items of Revenue Expenditure	**Assets**	**Items of Revenue Income**
Advertising	Bills Receivable	Bad Debts Recovered
Bad Debts	Cash at Bank	Commission Received
Bank Interest Paid	Cash in Hand	Discount Received
Bill Discount	Debtors	Dividends Received
Carriage Inwards	Fixtures and Fittings	Purchases Returns or
Carriage Outwards	Goodwill	Returns Out
Commission Paid	Land and Buildings	Royalties Received
Customs Duty	Loan to a Person	Sales — Cash and Credit
Depreciation	Loose Tools	
Discount Allowed	Motor Vehicles	**Liabilities**
Dividends Paid	Patents and Trade Marks	Bank Overdraft
Electricity	Plant and Machinery	Bills Payable
Entertaining Expenses	Stock	Capital
Gas	Work in Progress	Current Account —
Insurance		Unless Overdrawn
Loan Interest Paid	**Other**	Creditors
Motor Expenses	Personal Drawings	Loan from a Person
Motor Licences		PAYE due to be Paid
Office Expenses		Provision for Bad Debts
Packing		
Power		
Purchases — Cash and Credit		
Rates		
Rent		
Repairs to Plant		
Salaries		
Sales Returns or Returns In		
Stationery		
Sundry Expenses		
Telephone		
Travelling Expenses		
Wages		
Water		

Suspense Account

Purpose   A Suspense Account is opened where a difference occurs in a Trial Balance caused by the incomplete recording of the double-entry in respect of one or more transactions. The difference is recorded in the Suspense Account and entered in the Trial Balance so agreeing it. When the difference is found this will eliminate the balance on the Suspense Account.

Instructions   *To Corrrect Errors by using a Suspense Account*
1 The difference in the Trial Balance is recorded in the Suspense Account and the balance on the latter Account entered in the Trial Balance.
2 The reason for the difference in the Trial Balance has to be found by checking through the entries in the books.
3 The entries to adjust the difference have to be recorded through the Journal and posted to the Suspense Account and the relevant ledger accounts.
4 The Suspense Account will then be closed and the Suspense Account will be replaced by the amended balances.

Example   On 31 December the Trial Balance extracted from the books of A. Draper revealed the following position:

Totals after various accounts	**DR**	**CR**
have been listed	*£10,000*	*£ 4,550*
Sales		*5,000*
A. Brown		*250*
Difference		*200*
	£10,000	*£10,000*

After checking through the entries in the books it is found that
1 The Sales Day Book has been undercast by £300.
2 A cheque for £100, paid to A. Brown, had not been posted to his account in the Ledger.
You are required to adjust the errors in the books of A. Draper by using a Suspense Account.

Solution to Example on page 48

Step 1   *Open a Suspense Account to record the difference in the Trial Balance.*

DR	SUSPENSE ACCOUNT	CR
	Dec 31 Difference in Trial Balance £200	

Record the Suspense Account Balance in Trial Balance.

TRIAL BALANCE as at 31 DECEMBER (before adjustments)

	DR	CR
Totals from various accounts have been listed	£10,000	£4,550
Sales		5,000
A. Brown		250
Suspense Account		200
	£10,000	£10,000

Step 2   The errors have been found to be:

a) The Sales Day Book has been undercast by £300.
b) A cheque for £100, paid to A. Brown, had not been posted to his account.

Step 3   Adjustments required to correct these errors:

a) An increase to be made in the Sales Day Book of £300.
b) A. Brown's Account to be debited with £100.

The Suspense Account after correction of errors would be:

DR		Suspense Account		CR
Dec. 31	Sales £300	Dec. 31	Difference in Trial Balance	£200
			A. Brown	100
	£300			£300

Step 4   After correction of errors the Trial Balance would appear:

TRIAL BALANCE as at 31 December (after adjustments)

	DR	CR
Totals from various accounts have been listed	£10,000	£4,550
*Sales		5,300
*A. Brown		150
	£10,000	£10,000

* These balances are now shown in their amended form. The Suspense Account is now closed.

Stock

Definition Stock represents purchases of goods for resale which have been made by a business and which have not been sold at the end of the financial period.

Instructions *To Record Stock in the Books of the Business*
Step 1 Check that the opening stock, if any, appears as a debit balance in the stock account.
2 Transfer the opening stock to the Trading Account at end of financial period.
3 Record closing stock as follows:
'DR' Stock Account
'CR' Trading Account
4 Record closing stock in Balance Sheet.

Example A. Draper has opening stock of £2,000 at 1 January and closing stock of £3,000 at 31 December, his financial year end.

Record the above in the books of A. Draper and show how the items would appear in

1 The Stock Account
2 The Trading Account
3 The Balance Sheet

Solution to Example on page 50
Step 1

DR			Stock Account			(S8)	CR
Jan 1	Balance	b/d	£2,000				

Step 2 Transfer Opening Stock to Trading Account

	Journal			(J1)	
Dec 31	Trading	DR	$\frac{IL}{T6}$	£2,000	
	To Stock (opening)		$\frac{IL}{S8}$		£2,000
	Transfer of opening stock				

DR			Stock Account			(S8)	CR
Jan 1	Balance	b/d	£2,000	Dec 31	Trading	J1	£2,000

DR			Trading Account			(T6)	CR
Dec 31	Stock	J1	£2,000				

Step 3 Recording Closing Stock and Transfer to Trading Account

	Journal			(J1)	
Dec 31	Stock (closing)	DR	$\frac{IL}{S8}$	£3,000	
	To Trading		$\frac{IL}{T6}$		£3,000
	Transfer of closing stock				

DR			Stock Account			(S8)	CR
Dec 31	Trading	J1	£3,000				

DR			Trading Account			(T6)	CR
Dec 31	Stock (opening)	J1	£2,000	Dec 31	Stock (closing)	J1	£3,000

Step 4	Balance Sheet (Extract)	
	Current Assets	
	Stock	£3,000

Prepaid Charges

Prepaid charges or expenses are amounts which have been paid before the expiration of the period to which they relate. To deal with this accounting problem the Expense Account is reduced by the unexpired amount and the latter sum treated as an asset in the Balance Sheet.

Instructions

Step 1 Find out if any amounts have been paid which cover a period beyond the end of the financial period.

2 Calculate the period still to expire after the financial period.

3 Calculate the amount of the prepaid charge.

4 Prepare Journal entry.

5 Record in Ledger Account and close off to Profit and Loss Account.

6 Show asset in Balance Sheet.

Example

The insurance account appears in the books of A. Draper as follows:

DR			Insurance Account				CR
June 30	Bank	CB 1	£300				

The payment made on June 30 is in respect of an insurance premium covering the period of one year. A. Draper makes up his annual accounts to 31 December.

Step 1

The insurance premium paid covers a period beyond the end of the financial year.

Step 2

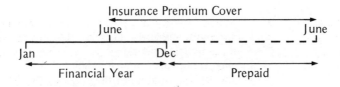

Step 3

Six months prepaid insurance is $\dfrac{£300}{2} = £150$

Step 4

Journal			(J1)		
Dec 31	Insurance – new period DR	$\dfrac{IL}{I3}$	£1 50	
	To Insurance – old period	$\dfrac{IL}{I3}$		£1 50
	Being six months' insurance premium prepaid to date			

Step 5

DR			Insurance Account				(I3)	CR
June 30	Bank	$\dfrac{CB}{1}$	£300	Dec 31	Prepaid	J1	£1 50
					Profit and		
					loss	J1	£1 50
			£300				£300
Jan 1	Prepaid	J1	£1 50				

Note:
A Journal entry would be required to transfer the balance of insurance account to profit and loss acount.

Profit and Loss Account (Extract)	
Insurance £1 50	

Step 6

Balance Sheet (Extract)	
	Current Assets
	Prepaid charge £1 50

Accrued Charges

Expenses which have been incurred for the period but have not been paid or recorded are known as *accrued* charges. It is necessary to adjust the relevant ledger accounts for these expenses so that the existing charge in the accounts is increased by the amount of the accrual and liability is recorded.

Instructions

Step 1 Find out if any amounts are due but unpaid at the end of financial period.
    2 Calculate the period outstanding.
    3 Calculate the amount of the accrual.
    4 Prepare Journal entry.
    5 Record in Ledger Account and close off to the Profit and Loss Account.
    6 Show liability in Balance Sheet.

Example

A. Draper has rented a warehouse for storage purposes at £200 per year. The rent is payable in arrears at 30 June and 31 December. At 31 December, the end of his financial year, the rent account was as follows:

DR			Rent Account				CR
June 30	Bank	CB 1	£100				

The December payment for rent had not been made at the end of the financial year.

Step 1
Rent is due and unpaid at end of year

Step 2

Financial Year

Step 3
Six months rent is $\dfrac{£200}{2} = £100$

Step 4

	Journal				(J1)
Dec 31	Rent — old period DR	$\dfrac{IL}{R6}$	£100		
	To Rent — new period	$\dfrac{IL}{R6}$		£100	
	Being rent due and unpaid at end of year				

Step 5

DR				Rent Account		(R6)	CR
June 30	Bank	CB 1	£100	Dec 31	Profit and Loss	J1	£200
Dec 31	Accrued	J1	100				
			£200				£200
				Jan 1	Accrued	J1	£100

Note: A Journal entry would be required to transfer the balance of rent account to profit and loss account.

Profit and Loss Account (Extract)		
Rent	£200	

Step 6

Balance Sheet (Extract)	
Current Liabilities Accrued Charge £100	

Bad Debts

Purpose

If a debtor is unable to pay the amount owing, this amount is treated as a bad debt and is written off to Profit and Loss Account as a business expense.

Instructions

To Write off a Debtor's Account as a Bad Debt
Step 1 Close debtor's account and transfer to bad debts account.
     2 Write off bad debts account to profit and loss account at end of financial year.

Example

R. White owes £50 to A. Draper and is unable to make payment due to insolvency. His ledger account appears as follows:

DR				R. White Account		(W6)	CR
Jan 1	Balance	b/d	£50				

A. Draper decides to write off the debt as bad on 31 December, his financial year end.

Step 1

	Journal			(J1)	
Dec 31	Bad debts DR	$\frac{\text{IL}}{\text{B7}}$	£50	
	To R. White	$\frac{\text{SL}}{\text{W6}}$		£50
	Debt written off as bad			

DR		Bad Debts Account			(B7)			**CR**
Dec 31	R. White	J1	£50					

DR		R. White Account			(W6)			**CR**
Jan 1	Balance	b/d	£50	Dec 31	Bad debts	J1	£50	

Step 2

	Journal				
Dec 31	Profit and loss DR	$\frac{\text{IL}}{\text{P7}}$	£50	
	To Bad debts	$\frac{\text{IL}}{\text{B7}}$		£50
	Being bad debts written off			

DR		Bad Debts Account			(B7)			**CR**
Dec 31	R. White	J1	£50	Dec 31	Profit and loss	J1	£50	

DR		Profit and Loss Account			(P7)			**CR**
Dec 31	Bad debts	J1	£50					

Provision for Bad Debts

A bad debts provision arises where it is considered prudent to make provision for debts which are doubtful as to payment but not necessarily bad.

Instructions

Step 1 Decide on the amount of the provision required.

2 Create the provision for bad debts by transferring the agreed amount from profit and loss account.

3 Show the provision as a deduction from debtors in the Balance Sheet.

Example

A. Draper has total debtors of £10,000 at 31 December which is his financial year end. He decides to create a provision for bad debts amounting to 5% of total debtors.

Step 1
Amount of provision is 5% x £10,000 = £500

Step 2

Journal			(J1)		
Dec 31	Profit and loss DR	$\frac{IL}{P7}$	£500	
	To Provision for bad debts	$\frac{IL}{P8}$		£500
	Being provision of 5% of debtors created this date.			

DR					Provision for Bad Debts Account		(P8)		CR
					Dec 31	Profit and loss	J1	£500

DR				Profit and Loss Account		(P7)		CR
Dec 31	Provision for bad debts	J1	£500				

Step 3

Balance Sheet (Extract)	
	Current Assets
	Debtors £10,000
	Less: provision
	for bad debts 500 **£9,500**

Depreciation
(STRAIGHT LINE METHOD)

Purpose   Many fixed assets wear out or become obsolete with the pass-
            age of time and must eventually be replaced. The loss in value
            of a fixed asset which must be taken into account in the busi-
            ness records is called *Depreciation*.

Causes of   Physical deterioration — Caused by wear and tear when the
Depreciation   asset is in use.
            Obsolescence   — Caused by asset becoming obsolete
                        or out of date due to new inventions
                        or improved methods.
            Inadequacy   — Caused by the growth and changes in
                        the business which makes the asset
                        incapable of achieving increased
                        service to the business.

Calculation of The following steps have to be taken:
Depreciation   1 Estimate the number of years of the asset's life.
(Straight Line 2 Assess its scrap value at the end of that period.
Method)   3 Deduct the scrap value from the cost.
            4 Divide the cost of the asset less scrap value by the estimated
               life of the asset in years.
            5 The formula would then be:

$$\frac{Cost - Scrap\ value}{Estimated\ life\ of\ asset\ in\ years} = \text{Annual depreciation charge.}$$

Instructions   *To write off depreciation*

            Step 1 Calculate amount of Depreciation to be written off.
                2 Write off Depreciation from Asset Account.
                3 Transfer Depreciation charge from Asset Account to
                   Profit and Loss Account.
                4 In the Balance Sheet show the balance of the Asset
                   Account at the start of the year less the annual charge for
                   Depreciation.

Example   A. Draper purchases fixtures costing £8,800 on January 1. He
            estimates the life of the fixtures will be ten years and the scrap
            value £800 at the end of that period. He decides that deprecia-
            tion should be written off over the life of the fixtures. His
            financial years ends on 31 December. Write up the Asset
            Account and show the amounts which would appear in the
            Profit and Loss Account and Balance Sheet for the first two
            years of the asset's life.

Solution to Example on page 60

Step 1	Calculation of Annual Depreciation Charge

$$\frac{Cost - Scrap\ Value}{Estimated\ life\ of\ assets\ in\ years} \quad \frac{8,800 - 800}{10} = \underline{\underline{£800}}$$

Step 2 **Write off Depreciation from Fixtures Account**

DR		Fixtures Account		CR
Year 1		Year 1		
Jan 1 Bank	£8,800	Dec 31 Profit and Loss	£800	
		Balance	8,000	
	£8,800		£8,800	
Year 2		Year 2		
Jan 1 Balance	8,000	Dec 31 Profit and Loss	800	
		Balance	7,200	
	£8,000		£8,000	
Year 3				
Jan 1 Balance	£7,200			

Step 3 **Transfer Annual Depreciation Charge to Profit and Loss Account**

Profit and Loss Account

Year 1		
Dec 31 Fixtures —		
Depreciation	£800	
Year 2		
Dec 31 ,,	£800	

Step 4 **Balance Sheet Position after providing for Depreciation**

Balance Sheet as at 31 December

Year 1 Fixtures	£8,800	
Less: Depreciation	800	£8,000
Year 2 Fixtures	£8,000	
Less: Depreciation	800	£7,200

Notes: 1 A Journal Entry would be required to transfer the Depreciation charge from the Fixtures Account to Profit and Loss Account.

2 An alternative method to record the Depreciation Charge would be to post it to a separate Fixtures Depreciation Account. Under this method the Fixtures Account would remain at the cost value of £8,800. Under this method the balance sheet presentation for year 2 would be:

Fixtures	£8,800	
Less: Depreciation to Date	1,600	£7,200

Depreciation
(REDUCING BALANCE METHOD)

Purpose   See page 60

Advantages of   . Commonly used in small businesses where it is difficult to
this method   obtain original cost of asset and date of purchase.
      . In this method depreciation charges are high in the initial
      years and repair costs light while in later years when repairs
      tend to rise the depreciation charge decreases.
      . Simple to operate when the life of the asset cannot be
      estimated with reasonable accuracy.

Calculation of   The following steps have to be taken:
Depreciation
(Reducing   1 Ascertain the cost of the Asset.
Balance   2 Estimate the number of years of the asset's life.
Method)   3 Assess the scrap value at the end of that period.
      From the above information the fixed percentage which will
      write down the amount to its estimated scrap value over the
      required number of years can be found from the formula:

$$r = \left(1 - \sqrt[n]{\frac{s}{c}}\right) 100$$

Where r is the desired rate, n the number of years of expected
asset life, s the expected scrap value and c the cost of the asset.

Instructions   *To write off Depreciation:*
      Step 1 Calculate amount of depreciation to be written off.
      2 Write off depreciation from Asset Account.
      3 Transfer Depreciation charge from Asset Account to
      Profit and Loss Account.
      4 In the Balance Sheet show the balance of the Asset
      Account at the start of the year less the annual charge
      for depreciation.

Example   A. Draper purchases fixtures costing *£8,800* on January 1. He
      estimates that the required rate of depreciation to be written
      off taking into account scrap value should be 20% per annum
      on the reducing balance method. His financial year ends on 31
      December. Write up the Asset Account and show the amounts
      which would appear in the Profit and Loss Account and
      Balance Sheet for the first two years of the asset's life.

Note: **Causes of Depreciation** See page 60.

Solution to example on page 62

Step 1   **Calculation of Annual Depreciation Charge**

	Year 1	20% X 8,800	= £1,760
	Year 2	20% (8,800 − 1,760)	= £1,408

Step 2   **Write off Depreciation from Fixtures Account**

DR			Fixtures Account		CR
Year 1			Year 1		
Jan 1 Bank		£8,800	Dec 31 Profit and Loss		£1,760
			Balance		7,040
		£8,800			£8,800
Year 2			Year 2		
Jan 1 Balance		7,040	Dec 31 Profit and Loss		1,408
			Balance		5,632
		£7,040			£7,040

Step 3   **Transfer Annual Depreciation Charge to Profit and Loss Account**

Profit and Loss Account

Year 1		
Dec 31 Fixtures −		
Depreciation	£1,760	
Year 2		
Dec 31 ,,	£1,408	

Step 4   **Balance Sheet Position after providing for Depreciation**

Balance Sheet as at 31 December

Year 1 Fixtures	£8,000		£8,800	See Note 2	
Less: Depreciation	1,760	£7,040	1,760	£7,040	
Year 2 Fixtures	£7,040		£8,800		
Less: Depreciation	1,408	£5,632	3,168	£5,632	

Notes: 1. A Journal Entry would be required to transfer the Depreciation charge from the Fixtures Account to Profit and Loss Account.
       2. An alternative method to record the Depreciation charge would be to post it to a separate Fixtures Depreciation Account. Under this method the Fixtures Account would remain at cost value £8,800.

Trading Account

Purpose   The Trading Account is prepared to calculate the Gross Profit for each accounting period.

Main Features
. Trading Account is a Ledger Account.
. Gross Profit is the difference between purchases and sales after adjusting for stocks and returns.
. Shows the Gross Profit for a trading period.
. Can be prepared as an analysed account showing Gross Profit for each department or business activity.
. Gross Profit is transferred to the Profit and Loss Account.

Instructions   *To Write up a Trading Account*
Step 1 Close off appropriate accounts to Trading Account.
     2 Record stock at end.
     3 Calculate Gross Profit.

Example   A. Draper has balances on the following accounts at 31 December:
Purchases Dr. *£3,000*; Sales Cr. *£5,000*;
Sales returns Dr. *£500*;   Purchases returns Cr. *£300*;
Stock (opening) Dr. *£1,000*; Carriage inwards Dr. *£200*.

The stock (closing) at 31 December amounted to *£2,000*.

His financial year ends on 31 December.
Prepare a trading account from this information.

Solution to above Example

DR				Trading Account			(T6)	CR
Dec 31	Purchases	J1	£3,000	Dec 31	Sales	J1		£5,000
	Sales returns	J1	500		Purchases returns	J1		300
	Stock (Opening)	J1	1,000		Stock (Closing)	J1		2,000
	Carriage	J1	200					
	*Balance – Gross profit	c/d	2,600					
			£7,300					£7,300
				Dec 31	Balance	b/d		£2,600

Note:
*This balance is transferred to the Profit and Loss Account.

The following are the Journal Entries required to transfer the balances on the Accounts to the Trading Account.

Journal					(J1)
Dec 31	Trading DR	IL/T6	£4,700	
	To Purchases	IL/P1		£3,000
	Sales returns	IL/S2		500
	Carriage inwards	IL/C5		200
	Stock (Opening)	IL/S6		1,000
	Being transfers to Trading account			
Dec 31	Sales DR	IL/S1	£5,000	
	Purchases returns	IL/P2	300	
	To Trading	IL/T6		5,300
	Being transfers to Trading account			
Dec 31	Stock (Closing) DR	IL/S6	£2,000	
	To Trading	IL/T6		2,000
	Being transfer of Closing stock			

The following are the Ledger Accounts as they would appear after being closed off.

DR			Purchases Account		(P1)		CR
Dec 31	Balance	b/d	£3,000	Dec 31	Trading	J1	£3,000

DR			Sales Returns Account		(S2)		CR
Dec 31	Balance	b/d	£500	Dec 31	Trading	J1	£500

DR			Stock Account		(S6)		CR
Dec 31	Balance	b/d	£1,000	Dec 31	Trading	J1	£1,000
Dec 31	Trading	J1	£2,000				

DR			Sales Account		(S1)		CR
Dec 31	Trading	J1	£5,000	Dec 31	Balance	b/d	£5,000

DR			Purchases Returns Account		(P2)		CR
Dec 31	Trading	J1	£300	Dec 31	Balance	b/d	£300

DR			Carriage Inwards Account		(C5)		CR
Dec 31	Balance	b/d	£200	Dec 31	Trading	J1	£200

Trading Account (cont.)

Presentation of Trading Account in Final Accounts
- The Trading Account is not usually presented as a ledger account in *final account* form.
- Sales returns are deducted from sales.
- Purchases returns are deducted from purchases.
- The stock at end is deducted from purchases after adjusting for the Opening Stock.
- The period covered by the Trading Account is shown in the main heading.
- No folio references are required.

Example

Trading Account prepared from Trial Balance

Trial Balance (Extract) at 31 December		
	Dr.	Dr.
Sales		£5,000
Purchases	£3,000	
Sales returns	500	
Purchases returns		300
Stock (opening)	1,000	
Carriage inwards	200	

A. Draper had stock at 31 December of £2,000.

Example of Trading Account in Final Accounts using the figures in the previous example.

Trading Account for year ended 31 December					
Purchases	£3,000			Sales	£5,000	
Less: Returns	300	£2,700		*Less:* Returns	500	£4,500
Add: Opening stock		1,000				
		3,700				
Less: Closing stock		2,000	£1,700			
Carriage inwards			200			
Gross profit for year			2,600			
			£4,500			£4,500

The amount of £1,700 represents the cost of goods sold.

Trading Account shown in vertical form

Trading Account for year ended 31 December			
Sales		£5,000	
Less : Returns		500	£4,500
Less: **Cost of sales**			
Purchases	£3,000		
Less: Returns	300	2,700	
Add: Opening stock		1,000	
		3,700	
Less: Closing stock		2,000	
		1,700	
Carriage inwards		200	1,900
Gross Profit for year			**£2,600**

Notes:
1. Carriage inwards relates to carriage charges on purchases and usually appears in the Trading Account.
2. In some instances wages may be shown in the Trading Account as opposed to the Profit and Loss Account if it is considered more meaningful.

Profit and Loss Account

Purpose

The Profit and Loss Account is prepared to calculate the profit or loss for a period of trading. Profit is the surplus after charging all revenue expenses of the business against the gross profit and other revenue income. A loss arises if the expenses exceed the income.

Main Features

- . Profit and Loss Account is a Ledger Account.
- . Forms part of the Final Accounts of a business.
- . Shows the profit or loss for an accounting period.
- . Can be analysed to show the profit for each department or trading activity of a business.
- . Profit or loss for the period is transferred to the Capital Account of the owner.

Instructions

To Write up a Profit and Loss Account

Step 1 Transfer the Gross Profit from Trading Account to credit of Profit and Loss Account.

2 Adjust ledger accounts for accrued and prepaid charges, depreciation, bad debts or provision for bad debts as required.

3 Close off the Ledger Accounts to Profit and Loss Account.

4 Calculate profit or loss for period.

5 Transfer profit or loss to Capital Account of owner.

Example

A. Draper has balances on the following ledger accounts at 31 December which is his financial year end.

Trading account Cr. £2,600;   Wages Dr. £600;
Rent Dr.£100;   General expenses Dr. £50;
Discount received Cr. £60;   Capital Cr. £5,000.

Wages due and unpaid at 31 December amounted to £100.
Prepare a profit and loss account from this information.

(for continuation see next page)

The Ledger Accounts as they would appear after transfers to Profit and Loss Account have taken place.

DR			Trading Account		(T6)	CR
Dec. 31	Profit and loss	J1	£2,600	Dec. 31	Balance b/d	£2,600

DR			Wages Account		(W5)	CR
Dec. 31	Balance b/d	£600	Dec. 31	Profit and loss	J1	£700
	Accrued J1	100				
		£700				£700
			Jan 1	Accrued	J1	£100

DR			Rent Account		(R3)	CR
Dec. 31	Balance	b/d	£100	Dec. 31	Profit and loss J1	£100

DR			General Expenses Account		(G4)	CR
Dec. 31	Balance	b/d	£50	Dec. 31	Profit and loss J1	£50

DR			Discount Received Account		(D3)	CR
Dec. 31	Profit and loss	J1	£60	Dec. 31	Balance b/d	£60

DR			Capital Account		(C4)	CR
Dec. 31	Balance	c/d	£6,810	Dec. 31	Balance b/d	£5,000
					Profit and loss J1	1,810
			£6,810			£6,810
				Jan 1	Balance b/d	£6,810

The Journal entries required to transfer the balances on the Ledger Accounts to Profit and Loss Account.

Journal			(J1)	
Dec. 31	Trading DR	IL/T6	£2,600	
	To Profit and Loss	IL/P7		£2,600
	Being transfer of Gross Profit			
Dec. 31	Wages — Old DR	IL/W5	£100	
	To Wages — New	IL/W5		£100
	Being accrual of wages at date			
Dec. 31	Profit and Loss DR	IL/P7	£850	
	To Wages	IL/W5		£700
	Rent	IL/R3		100
	General Expenses	IL/G4		50
	Being transfers to Profit and Loss			
Dec. 31	Discount received DR	IL/D3	£60	
	To Profit and Loss	IL/P7		£60
	Being transfer to Profit and Loss			
Dec. 31	Profit and Loss DR	IL/P7	£1,810	
	To Capital	IL/C4		£1,810
	Being transfer of Profit for year			

Profit and Loss Account (cont.)

Example (cont'd.) The Profit and Loss Account opposite refers to previous example on page 69.

Presentation *Presentation of Profit and Loss Account in final accounts*
.   The Profit and Loss Account is not usually presented as a Ledger Account in the final account form.
.   Adjustments for accrued and prepaid charges are not shown separately as these have been made in the Ledger Accounts.
.   The period covered by the Profit and Loss Account is shown in the main heading.
.   No folio references are required.

Example *Profit and Loss Account prepared from Trial Balance*

Trial Balance (Extract) at 31 December		
	Dr.	Cr.
Trading Account— Gross Profit		£2,600
Wages (inc. accrued £100)	£700	
Rent	100	
General expenses	50	
Capital — A. Draper		5,000

The Profit and Loss Account in Ledger form would appear thus:

DR				Profit and Loss Account		(P7)	CR
Dec. 31	Wages	J1	£ 700	Dec. 31	Trading	J1	£2,600
	Rent	J1	100		Discount received	J1	60
	General expenses	J1	50				
	Capital	J1	1,810				
			£2,660				£2,660

Example of Profit and Loss Account prepared from Trial Balance in Final Accounts form.

Profit and Loss Account for year ended 31 December

Wages	£700	Gross Profit	£2,600
Rent	100	Discount Received	60
General Expenses	50		
Profit for year	1,810		
	£2,660		£2,660

Profit and Loss Account shown in Vertical Form

Profit and Loss Account for year ended 31 December

Gross Profit		£2,600
Add: Discount received		60
		2,660
Less: Wages	£700	
Rent	100	
General Expenses	50	850
Profit for year		**£1,810**

Classification of Profit and Loss Account

Purpose

Classification of Accounts in Profit and Loss Account
Although the items shown in the Profit and Loss Account
are broadly classified as Revenue Expenses and Revenue
Income it is useful for the purpose of analysing and
interpreting the profit or loss brought out in this account
that the Revenue Expenses should be shown under main headings:

. **Administration expenses.**
. **Selling expenses.**
. **Finance expenses.**

Examples

Administration expenses
These relate to the overall expenses of running the office
and the operation of the business generally but are not part
of the actual selling expenses.
Examples
Office salaries
Rent, rates and insurance
Heating and lighting
Printing and stationery
Legal expenses
Audit fees
Telephone and postages
Depreciation of office assets
General office expenses

Selling expenses
These relate to the costs directly connected with making
sales and performing the sales activities.
Examples
Salesmen's salaries and commission
Travelling expenses of salesmen
Advertising
Carriage outwards
Bad debts

Finance expenses
These are expenses incurred as a result of borrowing money
or for credit extended to the business.
Examples
Bank overdraft interest
Loan interest
Discount allowed

Example of Analysed Profit and Loss Account in Vertical Form

A. Draper
Profit and Loss Account for year ended 31 December

Gross profit for year			£32,000
Add: **Sundry receipts**			
Discount received		£590	
Commission received		30	
Dividends received		50	670
			32,670
Less: **Administration expenses**			
Office salaries	£1,500		
Insurance	200		
Light and heat	300		
Rent and rates	1,200		
Audit fee	100	£3,300	
Selling expenses			
Salaries of salesmen	£6,500		
Delivery vehicle expenses	2,000		
Travelling expenses	350	£8,850	
Finance expenses			
Discount allowed	£600		
Bank interest	700	£1,300	13,450
Profit for year			**£19,220**

Balance Sheet

Purpose

It is one of the most important financial accounting statements which reveals the overall financial position of a business and discloses information about the assets and liabilities of the business and the amount of owner's capital invested in it.

Main Features

. Balance Sheet forms part of the Final Accounts of a business.
. It is *not* a ledger account but a statement of assets, liabilities and the owner's capital.
. It is a financial statement prepared 'As At' a particular point in time.
. Normally assets are shown on the right hand side.
. Normally liabilities and the owner's capital appear on the left hand side.
. Total assets equal liabilities plus owner's capital.

Main Headings

Assets
Basically assets are things of value usually of a tangible nature.
Examples
Property, plant, motor cars, stock, debtors, cash.

Liabilities
These are amounts owed by a business.
Examples
Creditors, bank overdraft, loans to the business, mortgages.

Capital
This is the excess of assets over liabilities which equals investment by the owner of the business.
Example
Owner's capital.

Example of a Balance Sheet

Balance Sheet as at 31 December

Capital		£5,000	Assets	
Liabilities			Motor car	£1,000
Creditors	£2,000		Stock	3,500
Bank overdraft	1,000	3,000	Debtors	3,000
			Cash	500
		£8,000		**£8,000**

From the above Balance Sheet it will be seen that:

Assets = Liabilities + Capital

This Balance Sheet equation may be expressed in another way

Assets − Liabilities = Capital

This equation can be proved by showing the Balance Sheet in vertical form.

Assets		
Motor car		£1,000
Stock		3,500
Debtors		3,000
Cash		500
		£8,000
Less: **Liabilities**		
Creditors	£2,000	
Bank overdraft	1,000	3,000
		£5,000
Represented by		
Capital		**£5,000**

Preparation of a Balance Sheet

To Write up Balance Sheet
The balances remaining after completing the Trading and
Profit and Loss Accounts are listed under the headings
assets, liabilities and capital.

To Illustrate the Preparation of a Balance Sheet
1 D. Brown commenced business on 1 January with capital
   of *£1,000* which was paid into the business Bank account.
2 On 2 January D. Brown purchased a motor car by cheque
   for *£500*. On the same date he received a loan of £600 from
   C. White to assist in the expansion of his business.
   The amount was paid by cheque.

Preparation of a Balance Sheet

Example 1

DR		Bank Account			CR
Jan 1	Capital	£1,000			

DR		Capital Account			CR
			Jan 1	Bank	£1,000

If a Balance Sheet is drawn up on 1 January after recording this transaction it will appear thus:

Balance Sheet as at 1 January			
Capital	£1,000	Assets — Bank	£1,000

Example 2

DR		Bank Account			CR
Jan 1	Capital	£1,000	Jan 2	Motor car	£500
				Balance	1,100
2	Loan C. White	600			
		£1,600			£1,600

DR		Capital Account			CR
			Jan 1	Bank	£1,000

DR		Motor Car Account			CR
Jan 2	Bank	£500			

DR		Loan Account — C. White			CR
			Jan 2	Bank	£600

If a Balance Sheet is drawn up after transactions have been recorded it will appear thus:

Balance Sheet as at 2 January			
Capital	£1,000	Assets	
		Motor car	£500
Liabilities		Bank	1,100
Loan — C. White	600		
	£1,600		£1,600

Preparation of a Balance Sheet (cont.)

Further Divisions

Assets are further classified as:
Fixed Assets
These are made up of items which are likely to remain
in the business over a long period and are basically acquired
to be used for the benefit of the business over a number of
years rather than sold again at a profit.

Current Assets
These are constantly turning over in the day-to-day
operations of the business and are easily converted into
cash.

Liabilities are further classified as:
Long-term Liabilities
These are amounts advanced to the business on a long term
basis normally for a period exceeding a year.

Current Liabilities
These are liabilities which are to be settled within a short
period of time but no longer than one year from the
Balance Sheet date.

Capital

The Capital Account is usually expanded to show the
capital balance brought forward from the previous period
with the current profits for period added to it and any
personal drawings of the owner deducted.

Example of a Balance Sheet showing the further Classifications

Balance Sheet as at 31 December

Capital			Fixed Assets		
Opening balance	£15,000		Land		£ 1,000
Add: Profit	1,000		Buildings		2,000
	———		Plant	£4,000	
	16,000		*Less:* Depreciation	2,500	1,500
Less: Drawings	500	£15,500	Furniture and	———	
	———		fittings		300
Long-term Liabilities			Motor cars		2,200
Mortgage		3,000			———
					7,000
Current Liabilities			**Current Assets**		
Short-term loan	£ 600		Stock	£8,000	
Creditors	3,400	4,000	Debtors	6,000	
	———		Prepaid charges	400	
			Cash at bank	1,000	
			Cash on hand	100	15,500
		———			———
		£22,500			£22,500

Note: Bank overdraft would be shown as a Current Liability where appropriate. Shown in vertical form the above Balance Sheet would appear thus:

Balance Sheet as at 31 December

Fixed Assets		
(Detail)		£X
Current Assets		
(Detail)	£X	
Less: **Current Liabilities**		
(Detail)	X	X
	———	———
		£X
		═══
Represented by:		
Capital — (Detail)		£X
Long-term Liabilities — (Detail)		X
		———
		£X
		═══

Bank Reconciliation Statement

Purpose

To agree the balance shown in the Bank column of the Cash Book with that recorded on the Bank statement.

Instructions

To Prepare a Bank Reconciliation Statement

Step 1   Enter Bank balance appearing in Cash Book at date of reconciliation.

    2   *Add/deduct† lodgements which have not been entered in Cash Book but appear on Bank statement.

    3   *Deduct/add† cheque payments not entered in Cash Book but appear on Bank statement.

    4   The resulting amount will be the adjusted Cash Book balance and should be short ruled.

    5   Enter Bank balance per Bank statement at date of reconciliation.

    6   *Add/deduct† lodgements in Cash Book but not yet through Bank statement.

    7   *Deduct/add† cheques entered through Cash Book but not yet recorded through Bank statement.

    8   The resulting amount will be the adjusted Bank statement balance and should be short ruled.

Notes:

a. The amounts appearing in Step 4 and Step 8 should be in agreement.

b. Adjustments marked (*) should be used when the Bank balance is not overdrawn.

c. Adjustments marked (†) should be used when the Bank account is overdrawn.

Example of Bank Reconciliation Statement

A. Draper
Bank Reconciliation Statement as at 31 December

Steps

1	**Balance in Bank per Cash Book**			£340
2	*Add:* Lodgement not entered in cash book but on bank statement			
	Dividends on shares			50
				390
3	*Less:* Cheque payments not entered in cash book but on bank statement			
	Payment to A.A.	£15		
	Bank interest	20		35
4	**Adjusted Cash Book Balance**			£355
5	**Balance per Bank Statement**			£400
	Add: Lodgement not yet credited in bank statement			105
				505
7	*Less:* Cheques drawn but not yet presented for payment			
	T. Smith Cheque No. 255	£40		
	W. Brown Cheque No. 256	110		150
8	**Adjusted Bank Statement Balance**			£355

Note: Figures have been introduced to assist in the understanding of the form of presentation.

Example   From the following information prepare the Bank Reconciliation statement as at 31 July.

1 A. Draper received the following bank Statement for the month of July.

A. Draper A/C No 00956210					NEW BANK OF SCOTLAND Glasgow		
SO = Standing Order. O/D = Overdrawn.							
Date	Detail	Ch. No.	Debit		Credit		Balance
19– July 1							£500 O/D
3		100	55				555 O/D
5	Lodgment				100		455 O/D
7		102	10				465 O/D
15	S.O.		20				485 O/D
20	Bank Charges		b	5			490 O/D
27		101	30				520 O/D
29		103	40				560 O/D
31	Dividend received				a	50	510 O/D

2 A. Draper's Cash Book appears as follows for July.

DR				Cash Book			CR
Date	Details	Bank	Date	Details	Ch. No.		Bank
19–			19–				
July 5	Sales	£100	July 1	Balance			£500
31	Sales	c 90		H. Brown	100		55
	Balance	525	5	J. Jones	101		30
			6	Gas	102		10
			15	Rates	S.O.		20
			26	W. Smith	103		40
			29	T. Black	104	d	60
		£715					£715
			Aug. 1	Balance			£525

Solution to example on page 82.

A. Draper
Bank Reconciliation Statement as at 31 July

Steps

1	**Bank Balance per Cash Book**	^{O}/D	**£525**
2	*Less:* Lodgement not entered in cash book but on bank statement		
	Dividend received	a	50
			475
3	*Add:* Amount not entered in cash book but on bank statement		
	Bank charges	b	5
4	**Adjusted Cash Book Balance**	^{O}/D	**£480**
5	**Balance per Bank Statement**	^{O}/D	**£510**
6	*Less:* Lodgement not yet credited in bank statement but through cash book	c	90
			420
7	*Add:* Cheque drawn but not yet presented for payment		
	T. Black CH. No. 104	d	60
8	**Adjusted Bank Statement Balance**	^{O}/D	**£480**

Note: In this example it is necessary to compare the entries in the Cash Book with the Bank Statement to establish these amounts which are outstanding before preparing the Bank Reconciliation Statement.

Value Added Tax

Purpose   To record entries involving V.A.T. in the Purchases Day Book and Purchases Returns Book and posting to the Ledgers.

Instructions   To record entries involving V.A.T. in Purchases Day Book and Purchases Returns Book.

Purchases Day Book	Purchases Returns Book
1 Enter cost inc. V.A.T. in total column	1 Enter credit amount inc. V.A.T. in total column
2 Record V.A.T. in a separate column	2 Record V.A.T. in a separate column
3 Record cost of Goods/Services ex V.A.T. in separate column	3 Record credit amount ex V.A.T. in separate column
4 Post total amount of each transaction inc. V.A.T. to personal account in ledger	4 Post total amount of each transaction inc. V.A.T. to personal account in ledger
5 At the end of month post: V.A.T. amount to Dr. of V.A.T. Account. Goods column total ex Goods column total ex V.A.T. to Dr. of Purchases Account.	5 At the end of month post: V.A.T. amount to Cr. of V.A.T. Account. Goods column total ex Goods column total ex V.A.T. to to Cr. of Purchases Returns A/C.

To record entries involving V.A.T. from Day Books to Ledgers.

Purchases Ledger
Post to personal accounts amounts **inc.** V.A.T.

Impersonal Ledger
Post to impersonal accounts amounts **ex** V.A.T.

Example   To illustrate the treatment of entries involving V.A.T. in the Purchases Day Book and Purchases Returns Book.
A. Draper had the following transactions in June
June 1 Bought 20 coats on credit from J. Jones £345 (inc. V.A.T. £45)
     5 Returned 6 coats to J. Jones value £115 (inc. V.A.T. £15)
V.A.T. rate is to be assumed at 15%.

Solution to Example on page 84

Purchases Day Book					PDB 1
Date	Details	Folio	Total	VAT	Amount (ex VAT)
June 1	J. Jones — 20 coats	J1 ❹	£345 ❶	❷ £45 ❺ $\frac{IL}{5}$	❸ £300 ❻ $\frac{IL}{3}$

Purchases Returns Book					PRB 1
Date	Details	Folio	Total	VAT	Amount (ex VAT)
June 5	J. Jones — Returned 6 coats	J1 ❹	£115 ❶	❷ £15 ❺ $\frac{IL}{5}$	❸ £100 ❻ $\frac{IL}{4}$

Purchases Ledger

DR				J. Jones Account		(J1)		CR
June 5	Returns	PRB 1	£115 ❹	June 1	Purchases	PDB 1	£345 ❹	

Impersonal Ledger

DR			Purchases Account	(3)		CR
June 30	Total from P.D.B.	PDB 1	£300 ❺			

DR			Purchases Returns Account			(4)		CR
				June 30	Total from P.R.B.	PRB 1	£100 ❺	

Example of Invoice involving VAT

A. Draper
10 Cotton Street
Coaltown
Vat. No. 257 2961 40

J.Jones
5 Nylon Street,
Silktown

Invoice No. 2350
Date   1 June 19-
Tax Point 1 June 19-

Quantity	Detail		Cost	V.A.T. Rate	V.A.T.
20	COATS VAT	TOTAL	£300 45 £345	15%	£45

TERMS NET 7DAYS

Note the VAT Account is shown on page 89.

Purpose	To record entries involving V.A.T. in the Sales Day Book and Sales Returns Book and posting to the Ledgers.
Instructions	To record entries involving V.A.T. in Sales Day Book and Sales Returns Book.

Sales Day Book	Sales Returns Book
1 Enter Sale inc. V.A.T. in total column	1 Enter Returns inc. V.A.T. in total column
2 Record V.A.T. in a separate column	2 Record V.A.T. in a separate column
3 Record value of sale ex V.A.T. in separate column	3 Record returns ex V.A.T. in a separate column
4 Post total amount of each transaction inc. V.A.T. to personal account in ledger	4 Post total amount of each transaction inc. V.A.T. to personal account in ledger
5 At the end of the month post: V.A.T. amount to Cr. of V.A.T. Account. Goods column total Goods column total ex V.A.T. to Cr. of Sales Account.	5 At the end of the month post: V.A.T. amount to Dr. of V.A.T. Account. Goods column total Goods column total ex V.A.T. to Returns Account.

To record entries involving V.A.T. from Day Books to Ledgers.

Sales Ledger
Post to personal accounts amounts **inc.** V.A.T.

Impersonal Ledger
Post to impersonal accounts amounts **ex** V.A.T.

Example	To illustrate the treatment of entries involving V.A.T. in the Sales Day Book and Sales Returns Book. A. Draper had the following transactions in June June 8 Sold 5 coats on credit to R. Green £230 (inc. V.A.T. £30) 12 R. Green returned 2 coats to A. Draper as faulty £92 (inc. V.A.T. £12) V.A.T. rate is to be assumed at 15%.

Solution to Example on page 86

Sales Day Book					SDB1
Date	Details	Folio	Total	VAT	Amount (ex. VAT)
June 8	R. Green — 5 coats	G1 ❹	£230 ❶	❷ £30 ❺ $\frac{IL}{5}$	❸ £200 ❻ $\frac{IL}{6}$

Sales Returns Book					SRB1
Date	Details	Folio	Total	VAT	Amount (ex. VAT)
June 12	R. Green — Returned 2 coats	G1 ❹	£92 ❶	❷ £12 ❺ $\frac{IL}{5}$	❸ £80 ❻ $\frac{IL}{7}$

Sales Ledger

DR			R. Green Account			(G1)	CR
June 8	Sales	SDB 1	£230 ❹	June 12	Returns	SRB 1	❹ £92

Impersonal Ledger

DR			Sales Account			(6)	CR
				June 30	Total from SDB	SDB 1	❺ £200

DR			Sales Returns Account			(7)	CR
June 30	Total from S.R.B.	SRB 1	❺ £80				

Example of Credit Note involving VAT

R. Green 6 Braid Street Wooltown VAT No. 354 9510 20	A.DRAPER 10 Cotton Street, Coaltown		CREDIT NOTE No. 35 Date 12 June – Tax Point 12 June	
Quantity	Detail	Cost	VAT Rate	VAT
2	COATS - FAULTY VAT TOTAL	£80 12 92	15%	£12

Note the VAT account is shown on page 89.

Purpose	To record entries involving V.A.T. in the Cash Book and posting to the Ledger.

Instructions   To record entries involving V.A.T. in the Cash Book.

Receipts	Payments
1 Enter receipt inc. V.A.T. in cash/bank colum	1 Enter payment inc. V.A.T. in cash/bank column
2 Enter V.A.T. in a separate column if the transaction has not been recorded in day book	2 Enter V.A.T. in a separate column if the transaction has not been recorded in day book
3 Record amount of above transaction ex V.A.T. in a separate column	3 Record amount of above transaction ex V.A.T. in a separate column
4 Post total of V.A.T. column to the 'CR' of V.A.T. Account	4 Post total of V.A.T. column to 'DR' of V.A.T. Account

To record entries involving V.A.T. from Cash Book to Ledgers.

Personal Ledger
Amounts received from debtors and creditors are posted inc. V.A.T.

Impersonal Ledger
Post to impersonal accounts amounts ex V.A.T.

Example	To illustrate the treatment of entries involving V.A.T. in the Cash Book.

A. Draper had the following transactions in June
June 15 Received from R. Green a cheque £138 being the balance of his account.
     17 Paid J. Jones by cheque £230 being the balance on his account.
     29 Bought by cheque a machine £575 (inc. V.A.T. £75) This transaction was not entered through the day book.
     30 Cash Sales for month amounted to £460 (inc. V.A.T. £60) and were lodged in Bank.
Assume rate of V.A.T. to be 15%.

Solution to Example on page 88.

DR										Cash Book						Folio CB1		CR

Cash Book — Folio CB1

Date	Detail	Folio	Bank	VAT	Amount (ex VAT)	Date	Detail	Folio	Bank	VAT	Amount (ex VAT)
June 15	R. Green	$\frac{SL}{G1}$	❶ £138			June 17	J. Jones	$\frac{PL}{J1}$	❶ £230		
30	Cash sales	$\frac{IL}{1}$	❶ 460	❷ £60	❸ £400	29	Machine	$\frac{IL}{2}$	❶ 575	❷ £75	❸ £500
	Balance	c/d	207								
			£805	£60	£400				£805	£75	£500
				$\frac{IL}{5}$ ❹		July 1	Balance	b/d	£207	$\frac{IL}{5}$ ❹	

Note that additional columns for discount and cash can be added as required.

Purchases Ledger

DR			J. Jones Account			(J1)		CR
June 17	Bank	CB/1	£230	June 17	Balance	b/d		£230

Sales Ledger

DR			R. Green Account			(G1)		CR
June 15	Balance	b/d	£138	June 15	Bank	CB/1		£138

Impersonal Ledger

DR			Cash Sales Account			(1)		CR
				June 30	Bank	CB/1		£400

DR			Machine Account			(2)		CR
June 29	Bank	CB/1	£500					

The V.A.T. Account incorporating the foregoing examples is as follows:

DR			V.A.T. Account			(5)		CR
June 30	Total from P.D.B.	$\frac{PDB}{1}$	❺ £45	June 30	Total from P.R.B.	$\frac{PRB}{1}$		❺ £15
	Total from S.R.B.	$\frac{SRB}{1}$	❺ 12		Total from S.D.B.	$\frac{SDB}{1}$		❺ 30
	Total from C.B.	$\frac{CB}{1}$	❹ 75		Total from C.B.	$\frac{CB}{1}$		❹ 60
					Balance	c/d		27
			£132					£132
July 1	Balance	b/d	£27					

The balance on this V.A.T. Account represents the amount due from the Customs and Excise to the business.

Worked Example

H. Mitchell started business on 1 July and introduced as his capital the following assets: motor car £1,000 and stock of goods £500. He also paid £600 into the business bank account.

During the month of July the following transactions took place:

July 1 A cheque was drawn for cash £200.
   3 Purchased on credit from T. Brown goods value £400.
   6 Cash purchases £100.
   8 Sold on credit goods value £150 to W. Black.
 12 Returned goods bought from T. Brown as faulty £50.
 15 Paid by cheque insurance premium £70.
 16 Sold on credit to R. White goods value £300.
 19 W. Black returned goods damaged in transit £20.
 20 Paid T. Brown the amount due to him by cheque, less discount £10.
 21 Purchased on credit from W. Smith goods £500.
 23 Sold on credit to C. Green goods £250.
 25 Received from W. Black a cheque for £125 in settlement of his account.
    The balance was treated as discount.
 26 Received commission in cash £30.
 27 H. Mitchell withdrew cash £60 for personal use.
 28 Cash sales amounted to £350.
 29 Paid £200 cash into bank.
 30 Paid wages in cash £120.
 31 Paid general expenses in cash £40.

You are required to:
a. Record the above transactions in the books of H. Mitchell.
b. Make the following adjustments at 31 July.
  i.   Accrue wages amounting to £15.
  ii. Prepay insurance by £60.
  iii. Depreciate the motor car by £20.
  iv. As C. Green has been made bankrupt the balance on his account has to be written off as a bad debt.
  v. Stock at end of July amounts to £1,200.
c. Close off the books at 31 July and prepare a Trading and Profit and Loss Account and Balance Sheet.

See following pages for the suggested solution.

Solution

DR											CR

Cash Book Folio CB1

Date	Details	Folio	Discount allowed	Cash	Bank	Date	Details	Folio	Discount received	Cash	Bank
July 1	Capital	J1			£600	July 1	Cash	(c)			£200
1	Bank	(c)		£200		6	Purchases	$\frac{IL}{4}$		£100	
25	W. Black	$\frac{SL}{B1}$	£5		125	15	Insurance	$\frac{IL}{5}$			70
26	Commission	$\frac{IL}{6}$		30		20	T. Brown	$\frac{PL}{B1}$	£10		340
28	Sales	$\frac{IL}{8}$		350		27	Personal drawings	$\frac{IL}{7}$		60	
29	Cash	(c)			200	29	Bank	(c)		200	
						30	Wages	$\frac{IL}{9}$		120	
						31	General expenses	$\frac{IL}{10}$		40	
							Balances	c/d		60	315
			£5	£580	£925				£10	£580	£925
Aug 1	Balances	b/d	$\frac{IL}{11}$	£60	£315				$\frac{IL}{12}$		

Purchases Day Book				Folio PDB1	
Date	Details	Folio	Amount	Amount	
July 3	T. Brown – Goods	$\frac{PL}{B1}$		£400	
21	W. Smith – Goods	$\frac{PL}{S1}$		500	
	Posted to	$\frac{IL}{4}$		£900	

Sales Day Book				Folio SDB1	
Date	Details	Folio	Amount	Amount	
July 8	W. Black – Goods	$\frac{SL}{B1}$		£150	
16	R. White – Goods	$\frac{SL}{W1}$		300	
23	C. Green – Goods	$\frac{SL}{G1}$		250	
	Posted to	$\frac{IL}{8}$		£700	

Purchases Returns Book				Folio PRB1
Date	Details	Folio	Amount	Amount
July 12	T. Brown — Faulty goods returned	$\frac{PL}{B1}$		£50
	Posted to	$\frac{IL}{13}$		£50

Sales Returns Book				Folio SRB1
Date	Details	Folio	Amount	Amount
July 19	W. Black — Goods damaged in transit	$\frac{SL}{B1}$		£20
	Posted to	$\frac{IL}{14}$		£20

Purchases Ledger

DR			T. Brown Account			Folio B1	CR
July 12	Returns	$\frac{PRB}{1}$	£50	July 3	Purchases	$\frac{PDB}{1}$	£400
20	Bank	$\frac{CB}{1}$	340				
	Discount	$\frac{CB}{1}$	10				
			£400				£400

DR			W. Smith Account			Folio S1	CR
July 31	Balance	c/d	£500	July 21	Purchases	$\frac{PDB}{1}$	£500
				Aug 1	Balance	b/d	£500

Sales Ledger

DR				W. Black Account			Folio B1	CR
July 8	Sales	$\frac{SDB}{1}$	£150	July 19	Returns	$\frac{SRB}{1}$	£20
				25	Bank	$\frac{CB}{1}$	125
					Discount	$\frac{CB}{1}$	5
			£150				£150

DR				R. White Account			Folio W1	CR
July 16	Sales	$\frac{SDB}{1}$	£300	July 31	Balance	c/d	£300
Aug 1	Balance	b/d	£300				

DR				C. Green Account			Folio G1	CR
July 23	Sales	$\frac{SDB}{1}$	£250	July 31	Bad debts	J1	£250

Impersonal Ledger

DR				Capital Account			Folio 1	CR
July 31	Personal drawings	J1	£60	July 1	Sundries	J1	£2,100
	Balance	c/d	2,400	31	Profit and loss	J1	360
			£2,460				£2,460
				Aug 1	Balance	b/d	£2,400

DR				Motor Car			Folio 2	CR
July 1	Capital	J1	£1,000	July 31	Profit and loss	J1	£20
					Balance	c/d	980
			£1,000				£1,000
Aug 1	Balance	b/d	£980				

Impersonal Ledger (cont'd)

Stock Account — Folio 3

DR							CR
July 1	Capital	J1	£500	July 31	Trading	J1	£500
31	Trading	J1	£1,200				

Purchases Account — Folio 4

DR							CR
July 6	Cash	CB 1	£100	July 31	Trading	J1	£1,000
31	Total from P.D.B.	PDB 1	900				
			£1,000				£1,000

Insurance Account — Folio 5

DR							CR
July 15	Bank	CB 1	£70	July 31	Prepaid	J1	£60
					Profit and loss	J1	10
			£70				£70
Aug 1	Prepaid	J1	£60				

Commission Account — Folio 6

DR							CR
July 31	Profit and loss	J1	£30	July 26	Cash	CB 1	£30

Personal Drawings Account — Folio 7

DR							CR
July 27	Cash	CB 1	£60	July 31	Capital	J1	£60

Sales Account — Folio 8

DR							CR
July 31	Trading	J1	£1,050	July 28	Cash	CB 1	£350
				31	Total from S.D.B.	SDB 1	700
			£1,050				£1,050

DR			Wages Account		Folio 9	CR
July 30	Cash	CB 1	£120	July 31	Profit and loss	J1	£135
31	Accrued	J1	15				
			£135				£135
				Aug 1	Accrued	J1	£15

DR			General Expenses Account		Folio 10	CR
July 31	Cash	CB 1	£40	July 31	Profit and loss	J1	£40

DR			Discount Allowed Account		Folio 11	CR
July 31	Total from C.B.	CB 1	£5	July 31	Profit and loss	J1	£5

DR			Discount Received Account		Folio 12	CR
July 31	Profit and loss	J1	£10	July 31	Total from C.B.	CB 1	£10

DR			Purchases Returns Account		Folio 13	CR
July 31	Trading	J1	£50	July 31	Total from P.R.B.	PRB 1	£50

DR			Sales Returns Account		Folio 14	CR
July 31	Total from S.R.B.	SRB 1	£20	July 31	Trading	J1	£20

DR			Bad Debts Account		Folio 15	CR
July 31	C. Green	J1	£250	July 31	Profit and loss	J1	£250

Impersonal Ledger (cont'd)

DR				Trading Account				Folio 16	CR
July 31	Stock	J1	£500	July 31	Stock	J1	£1,200
	Purchases	J1	1,000		Sales	J1	1,050
	Sales returns	J1	20		Purchases returns	J1	50
	Profit and loss	J1	780				
			£2,300				£2,300

DR				Profit and Loss Account				Folio 17	CR
July 31	Wages	J1	£135	July 31	Trading	J1	£780
	Insurance	J1	10		Commission	J1	30
	General expenses	J1	40		Discount received	J1	10
	Discount allowed	J1	5				
	Motor car depreciation	J1	20				
	Bad debts	J1	250				
	Capital	J1	360				
			£820				£820

Journal			J1	
Date	Details	Folio	Amount	Amount
July 1	Motor car DR	$\frac{IL}{2}$	£1,000	
	Stock	$\frac{IL}{3}$	500	
	Bank	$\frac{CB}{1}$	600	
	To Capital	$\frac{IL}{1}$		£2,100
	Being Capital introduced by H. Mitchell.			
July 31	Wages – Old period DR	$\frac{IL}{9}$	£15	
	To Wages – New period	$\frac{IL}{9}$		£15
	Being Wages accrued at date			
	Insurance – New period DR	$\frac{IL}{5}$	£60	
	To Insurance – Old period	$\frac{IL}{5}$		£60
	Being Insurance prepaid at date			
	Bad debts DR	$\frac{IL}{15}$	£250	
	To C. Green	$\frac{SL}{G1}$		£250
	Being Debt written off as bad			

Continued overleaf

Journal (Cont'd.)			J1	
Date	Details	Folio	Amount	Amount
July 31 (cont'd)	Trading DR To Stock Being transfer of Opening Stock	$\frac{IL}{16}$ $\frac{IL}{3}$	£500	 £500
	Stock DR To Trading Being transfer of Closing Stock	$\frac{IL}{3}$ $\frac{IL}{16}$	£1,200	 £1,200
	Capital DR To Personal drawings Being transfer of Personal Drawings	$\frac{IL}{1}$ $\frac{IL}{7}$	£60	 £60

	Trading DR
	
	   To Purchases
	
	     Sales Returns
	 Being transfers to Trading Account
		$\frac{IL}{16}$
		
		 $\frac{IL}{4}$
		
		 $\frac{IL}{14}$
			£1,020	
				
				 £1,000
				
				 20

	Sales DR Purchases returns To Trading Being transfers to Trading Account	$\frac{IL}{8}$ $\frac{IL}{13}$ $\frac{IL}{16}$	£1,050 50	 £1,100

Journal (Cont'd.)				J1
Date	Details	Folio	Amount	Amount
July 31 (cont'd.)	Trading DR	IL/16	£780	
	To Profit and Loss Being transfer of Trading Profit	IL/17		£780
	Profit and loss DR	IL/17	£460	
	To Wages	IL/9		£135
	Insurance	IL/5		10
	General expenses	IL/10		40
	Discount allowed	IL/11		5
	Motor car depreciation	IL/2		20
	Bad debts Being transfers to Profit and Loss	IL/15		250
	Commission DR	IL/6	£30	
	Discount received	IL/12	10	
	To Profit and Loss Being transfers to Profit and Loss	IL/17		£40
	Profit and loss DR	IL/17	£360	
	To Capital Being transfer of Profit for month	IL/1		£360

H. Mitchell — Trading and Profit and Loss Account for Month of July

Sales		£1,050	
Less: Returns		20	£1,030
Less: **Cost of goods sold**			
Purchases	£1,000		
Less: Returns	50	£950	
Add: Opening stock		500	
		1,450	
Less: Closing stock		1,200	250
Gross Profit			780
Add: Commission			30
Discount received			10
			820
Less: Wages		£135	
Insurance		10	
Discount allowed		5	
Bad debts		250	
General expenses		40	
Depreciation on motor car		20	460
	Profit for month		£ 360

Balance Sheet as at 31 July

Capital Account				**Fixed Assets**			
Introduced at 1 July	£2,100			Motor car	£1,000		
Add: Profit for				*Less:* Depreciation	20	£980	
month	360						
	2,460			**Current Assets**			
Less: Drawings	60	£2,400		Stock	£1,200		
				Debtor	300		
Current Liabilities				Prepaid charge	60		
Creditor	£ 500			Cash at Bank	315		
Accrued charge	15	515		Cash on hand	60	1,935	
		£2,915				£2,915	

BUSINESS TRANSACTIONS (page 1)

1 Describe a business transaction and give an example.
2 What is meant by the two-fold aspect of a business transaction?
3 Analyse the two-fold aspect of these transactions entered into by J. Smith:
a He buys goods for cash £50.
b He pays rent in cash £30.
c He sells goods for cash £100.

RECORDING CASH TRANSACTIONS (p.2)

4 What do you understand by the term double-entry accounting?
5 What is meant by the term folio in accounting?
6 Show, in detailed form, a ledger account which could be used to record rent.
7 Record the following transactions, in account form, in the books of A. Brown.
a) He pays £2,500 in cash as capital into the business.
b) He buys for cash goods value £400.
c) He sells goods for cash value £600.
d) He pays rent in cash £50.
e) He pays wages in cash £30.
f) He buys a motor car £1,600 for cash.

RECORDING CREDIT TRANSACTIONS (p.4)

8 What is a credit transaction in business? Give an example.
9 Describe the basic accounting system to record credit transactions.
10 Record the following transactions in C. White's books:
a) Bought goods on credit value £60 from R. Jack.
b) Sold goods on credit value £90 to B. Smart.

BALANCING ACCOUNTS (p.6)

11 Describe the method used in balancing a ledger account.
12 From the following information write up the ledger accounts and balance them:

Account	Debit Entries		Credit Entries	
Cash	Capital £1,500		Purchases	£600
	Sales	500	Wages	50
			Rent	30
Sales			Cash	70
			Cash	50
Purchases	Cash	800	Cash (Refund)	20

TRIAL BALANCE (p.6)

13 What is meant in accounting by the term trial balance and what does it prove?

14 The following balances have been extracted from the books of a business. Show how they would appear in a Trial Balance.
Debit Balances: Cash £20; Purchases £80; Motor Car £500;
Typewriter £90; Electricity £25.
Credit Balances:Capital £595;   Sales £120.

CLASSIFICATION OF BUSINESS TRANSACTIONS (p.8)

15 Why is it necessary to classify business transactions?

16 What do the following terms mean?
Assets, Liabilities, Expenses, Income and Capital.

17 How would you classify the following items:
Plant, Debtors, Sales, Wages, Carriage, Postages, Creditors, Land and Discount Received.

CAPITAL AND REVENUE EXPENDITURE (p.9)

18 Why is it necessary to distinguish between capital and revenue expenditure?

19 Define the terms capital expenditure and revenue expenditure and give two examples of each.

20 A small retail draper has made payment for the following items:
(a) Salaries
(b) New show-case for shop
(c) Electricity bill
(d) New Cash Register
(e) Postage Stamps
(f) Rent of Shop
Which items are capital expenditure and which are revenue expenditure? Give reasons.

DIVISIONS OF LEDGERS (p.10)

21 Accounts are classified under main headings. What are these headings and explain the types of Accounts included under them?

22 How would you classify the following Accounts:
(a) J. Smith — a debtor of the business
(b) Printing and Stationery
(c) Furniture and Fittings
(d) R. Brown — a creditor of the business
(e) Land
(f) Purchases

23 List the main divisions of the Ledger and state what information you would expect to be contained within these ledger divisions.

BOOKS OF ORIGINAL ENTRY (p.11)

24 List the books of original entry used in a double-entry accounting system.

25 What use is made of books of original entry in a system of accounting?

PURCHASES DAY BOOK (p.12)

26 How is trade discount treated in the Purchases Day Book?

27 What is the purpose of using a Purchases Day Book in a business?

28 Enter the following transactions in the Purchases Day Book and post to the appropriate ledger accounts.

Jan. 2 Purchased on credit from R. Smith — 2 Refrigerators @ £100 each

10 Purchased on credit from W. Wilson — 1 Radio @ £25 and 2 Tape Recorders @ £20 each

19 Purchased on credit from J. Bryce — 2 Record Cabinets @ £30 each Less Trade Discount 20%

25 Purchased on credit from R. Smith — 1 Cabinet @ £40

29 Show the rulings which may be used by a small garage proprietor who wishes to record his purchase invoices in an analysed Purchases Day Book.

SALES DAY BOOK (p.14)

30 Why are cash sales not recorded in the Sales Day Book?

31 What are the main features of the Sales Day Book?

32 Record the following credit transactions in the Sales Day Book and post to the appropriate Ledger Accounts.

Jan 6 Sold to B. East — 1 Television set @ £300

15 Sold to W. Green — 2 Radios @ £35 and 1 Camera @ £120

30 Sold to N. Smart — 1 Refrigerator @ £150 less 10% Trade Discount

31 Sold to W. Green — 1 Cabinet £50

33 Show the rulings of an analysed Sales Day Book which may be suitable for a farmer.

PURCHASES RETURNS BOOK (p.16)

34 What is the Purchases Returns Book used for in an accounting system?

35 Enter the following transactions in the Purchases Returns Book and post to the appropriate Ledger accounts:

Jan 18 Returned to R. Smith — 1 Refrigerator damaged @ £100

23 Returned to J. Bryce — 1 Record Cabinet faulty @ £30 less 20% Trade Discount.

SALES RETURNS BOOK (p.18)

36   What are the main features of the Sales Returns Book?

37   Enter the following transactions in the Sales Returns Book and post to the appropriate Ledger Accounts.

Jan 18 W. Green returned 1 Radio @ £35 as faulty.

31 N. Smart returned the Refrigerator @ £150 less 10% Trade Discount as damaged.

CASH BOOK (Two Column) (p.20)

38   Explain the main features of the two-column cash book.

39   Enter the transactions in a two-column cash book and balance both columns after recording the entries.

Dec 1 Cash Sales £60

5 Cheque received from A. Brown £150

8 Cash Sales £130

9 Wages Paid in Cash £30

12 Postages paid by cash £2

18 Personal drawings of owner by cheque £70

26 Purchases by cheque £65.

40   A. Black had the following cash book transactions in May.

May 1 The cash balance amounted to £60 and the cash at bank was £100.

8 Received from J. Smith (debtor) £80 by cheque

10 Received Interest in cash £20

12 Transferred £40 from cash to bank

18 Paid G. Green (creditor) £90 by cheque

25 Paid wages in cash £10.

Record these entries in a two-column cash book and post to the appropriate ledger accounts.

CASH BOOK (Three-Column) (p.22)

41   Why do discount columns in the cash book not form part of the double entry system?

42   List the entries required to record contra accounts in the Cash Book.

43   On 1 January A. Todd's books had the following cash book balances:

Cash in Hand   £50

Cash at Bank   £400

During January the following transactions took place:

Jan 2 Received cheque from A. Smith £80. He had deducted £2 cash discount.

6 Paid to P. Smith his Account in cash £14

7 Paid rent in cash £10

9 Transferred from bank to Cash £60

11 Paid C. White by cheque, his outstanding account £60 less 5% cash discount

14 Received cheque in payment of D. Green's Account £40, less 5% cash discount

16 Cash Sales £25

23 Cash Purchases £15

29 Paid W. Fox his outstanding account by cheque £80 less 5% discount.

Enter the above in A. Todd's Cash Book and balance the Cash Book at the end of the month.

44   R. Blue had the following cash book transactions in July:

July 1 Cash balance amounted to £100 and the cash at Bank was £10

2 Received from J. Brown (debtor) £80 by cheque. Discount allowed was £4.

6 Received interest in cash £10

18 Transferred from cash to bank £40

20 Paid D. Black (Creditor) £200 by cheque. Discount received was £5.

25 Paid wages in cash £30.

Enter the above transactions in the Cash Book of A. Todd and balance it. Then post to the Ledger.

PETTY CASH BOOK (Normal System) (p.26)

45   Why do businesses record small payments in a separate Cash Book?

46   Rule a Petty Cash Book that will record the total expenditure under the headings — Postage and Stationery, Travelling Expenses, Carriage, and Office Expenses and enter the following transactions:

Jan 1 Petty Cash in Hand £40

5 Bought stamps £3

7 Paid Bus Fares £2; Paper £1

9 Paid Carriage £3; paid Rail Fares £5; bought Envelopes £6

12 Paid for Postages £7; paid for Tea and Sugar £2

Balance the Petty Cash Book as on 12 January and bring down the balance.

PETTY CASH BOOK (Imprest System) (p.28)

47   What is the Imprest System? What are its main advantages?

48   Prepare the ruling of A. Smith's Petty Cash Book with analysis columns for Postage, Carriage, Office Cleaning and Stationery.

The Book is kept on the Imprest System, the imprest amount being £40 and you are required to:

(a) Enter the following transactions:

April 1	Balance in Hand	£40
	Paid for office cleaning	£2
	Paid carriage	£1
3	Bought stamps	£3
4	Paid window cleaning	£4
	Bought Stationery	£2

	Paid Carriage	£3
6	Bought stamps	£5
	Paid Office Cleaner	£6
7	Bought envelopes	£2
9	Received cheque to make up imprest amount.	

(b) Balance Petty Cash Book as on 9 April.

(c) Post the analysis totals to the Ledger

JOURNAL (p.30)

49 What function does the Journal have in an accounting system?

50 Give three different examples when the Journal is required to record transactions.

51 Record Journal entries for the following in the books of B. Owen:

(a) On 1 May he commenced business with £2,000 capital made up as follows: Premises £1,500, Plant £200 and Stock of Goods £300.

(b) On 20 May he purchased on credit additional plant for £600 from G. Gray.

52 On 31 December A. King has balances on the following accounts which have to be closed off to the Trading and Profit and Loss Accounts:

Purchases 'Dr'	£4,000
Sales 'Cr'	£7,000
Office	
Expenses 'Dr'	£1,000

Prepare the necessary journal entries.

PURCHASES LEDGER (p.34)

53 What type of information is recorded in the Purchases Ledger?

54 A. Brown had the following transactions in May:

May 4 Bought on credit from J. Smith Goods £50

7 Bought on credit from W. Green Goods £70

11 Returned faulty goods to J. Smith £10

15 Paid J. Smith the balance due to him by cheque

17 Paid W. Green a cheque £67, discount received £3.

Record the above in the Day Books and Cash Book and post to the Creditors' Accounts in the Purchases Ledger.

SALES LEDGER (p. 36)

55 What is the purpose of the Sales Ledger?

56 R. White has the following transactions in July:

July 6 Sold Goods on credit to D. Brown £100

10 Sold Goods on credit to R. Black £75

12 R. Black returned goods £20 as faulty

15 Received cheque from D. Brown being the amount due by him

17 Received cheque from R. Black £52, discount allowed to him was £3

Record the above in the Day Books and Cash Book and post to the Debtors' Accounts in the Sales Ledger.

PURCHASES LEDGER CONTROL ACCOUNT (p.38)

57 What is the purpose of a Purchases Ledger Control Account?
58 From what sources is information obtained for preparing a Purchases Ledger Control Account?
59 A business keeps a Purchases Ledger which is checked by means of a Control Account. For 19X3 the following information is available:

Total Creditors' balances at 1 January 19X3	£4,700
Purchases for Year	5,510
Purchases Returns	120
Cash Paid to Creditors	4,950
Discount Received	290
Transfer of debit balances in Sales Ledger to Purchases Ledger	95

You are required to:
(a) Write up the Control Account for 19X3,
(b) State the source from which each of the above figures would be ascertained,
(c) State what the balance of the Control Account represents.

SALES LEDGER CONTROL ACCOUNT (p.40)

60 What are the main advantages of preparing a Sales Ledger Control Account?
61 Prepare a specimen Sales Ledger Control Account for one month during which sales are made, allowances are given for returns, cash is received, discount allowed and a bad debt is written off.
62 From the following information prepare the Sales Ledger Control Account for 19X2 and show the closing total amount of Debtors' balances.

Total Debtors' balances 1 January 19X2	£3,680
Goods sold on credit during 19X2	7,550
Sales Returns during 19X2	350
Bad Debts	60
Cheques received from customers	7,140
Discount allowed to customers	320
Customers' cheques dishonoured	210

IMPERSONAL LEDGER (p.42)

63 List four items which would appear on the debit side of an Account in the Impersonal Ledger.
64 Describe the types of items which would appear on the credit side of an Account in the Impersonal Ledger.

65 How does the Impersonal Ledger differ from the Sales and Purchases Ledgers?

66 A. Black had the following transactions in July:

July 9 Paid rates by cheque £50
    12 Received interest in cash £20
    15 Paid electricity by cheque £80
    17 Cash purchases amounted to £5
    19 Cash sales amounted to £15.

Record these in the Cash Book and·Impersonal Ledger of A. Black.

BALANCING LEDGER ACCOUNTS (p.44)

67 Outline the procedure for balancing an account.

68 Explain the abbreviations b/d and c/d and when are they used?

69 The opening balance at 1 May on T. Smith's Account in J. Black's books was £60 at debit. T. Smith was a debtor of A. Black. During the months of May, June and July the following transactions took place:

May 7 Sold goods on credit to T. Smith £50
    12 Received cheque for £60 from T. Smith
June 8 T. Smith returned goods amounting to £5
    12 Received cheque from T. Smith £30
July 19 Sold goods on credit to T. Smith £70
    26 Received cheque for £15.

From the above prepare the Ledger Account of T. Smith and balance it at the end of each month. No other Accounts are required.

TRIAL BALANCE (p.46)

70 What type of errors are disclosed by a trial balance?

71 On which side of the trial balance would you record the following:

(a) An item of revenue expenditure
(b) An increase in an asset
(c) An item of revenue income
(d) An increase in a liability

72 List the type of errors which are not disclosed by a trial balance.

73 Prepare a trial balance from the following list of balances extracted from the books of J. Jones: Capital £6,400, Land and Buildings £5,000, Motor Vehicles £600, Personal Drawings £1,400, Stock £910, Bank Overdraft £96, Sales £14,260, Purchases £11,100, Motor Expenses £310, Sundry Expenses £106, Wages £1,560, Debtors £820, Creditors £1,210, Rates and Insurance £160.

SUSPENSE ACCOUNT (p.48)

74 What is the purpose of a Suspense Account?

75 Explain the procedure to correct errors by using a Suspense Account.

76 On 31 December the Trial Balance of A. Thom shows the debit side to be £60 greater than the credit. After checking the following errors were found:
(a) A cash payment for a typewriter amounting to £135 was posted to the cash book only.
(b) A cheque from B. Smith for £70 had not been posted to his account.
(c) The Purchases Day Book had been overcast by £120.
(d) A credit note for £5 had been recorded in Sales Returns Book but had not been posted to A. Black's Account.
You are required to show the Suspense Account to correct the entries.

STOCK (p.50)
77 How would you define the term stock?
78 J. Smart has opening stock of £5,000 on 1 January and closing stock of £7,000 on 31 December which is his financial year end.
You are required to write up the Stock Account and show the entries as they would appear in the Trading Account and Balance Sheet. No Journal entries are required to be shown.

PREPAID CHARGES (p.52)
79 Why is it necessary to make an adjustment to an Expense Account for an amount prepaid?
80 Explain the basic steps necessary to make the accounting entries to record a prepaid charge.
81 A business paid its annual insurance premium on premises in advance on 1 March 19X2 amounting to £200. Final accounts are prepared on 31 December. Show how the Insurance Account would appear at 31 December 19X2.

ACCRUED CHARGES (p.54)
82 How would you set about making an adjustment to an Expense Account where there was an amount due but unpaid?
83 How would an Accrued Charge appear in the Balance Sheet?
84 A business pays its rates amounting to £600 by cheque, the dates of payment being at the end of each quarter, viz. 31 March, 30 June, 30 September and 31 December. When Final Accounts were prepared on 31 December 19X3 the payment for the last quarter had not been made. Show how the Rates Account would appear at 31 December 19X3 after adjusting for the amount due but unpaid. No journal entries are required.

BAD DEBTS (p.56/58)
85 How are bad debts treated in the books of a business?
86 Explain the steps you would take to write off a Debtor's Account as bad.

87 On 1 January 19X3 the following balances stood in the books of T. Black:

Debtors   A. Blue   £50

                 C. Green   £80

During the year both debtors were declared insolvent and unable to pay their debts. It was agreed that the Accounts would be written off as bad. Show how these matters would be dealt with in Black's books and state the amount which would appear in the Profit and Loss Account for the year ended 31 December 19X3. No journal entries need be shown.

PROVISION FOR BAD DEBTS (p.58)

88 What is the difference between Bad Debts written off and a provision for bad debts?

89 Explain the steps necessary to create a provision for bad debts in the books of a business.

90 The debtors in the books of C. Down amount to £2,000 at 31 December. It is decided that a provision for bad debts of 5% of debtors be created at that date.

You are required to show the Journal Entry to create the provision and give the relevant Ledger Accounts. Show also how the provision for bad debts would appear in C. Down's Balance Sheet.

DEPRECIATION
(Straight Line Method) (p.60)

91 What is the purpose of providing for depreciation?

92 What are the main causes of depreciation?

93 How do you calculate the amount of depreciation to be written off under the straight line method?

94 A business purchased a machine on 1 January 19X2 for £2,080. The machine is expected to last five years and to have an estimated scrap value of £80 at the end of that time. Final Accounts are prepared annually on 31 December. Show how the Machine Account and the Profit and Loss Account would appear in the books for the years ended 31 December 19X2 and 19X3 and the entries in the Balance Sheet at 31 December 19X3.

DEPRECIATION
(Reducing Balance Method) (p.62)

95 Explain the advantages of using the reducing balance method of depreciation.

96 How do you calculate the amount of depreciation to be written off using the reducing balance method?

97 A business purchased a Van value £6,000 on 1 January 19X3. Depreciation is to be provided using the reducing balance method at the rate of 20% per annum. Show the entries which would appear in the Van Account, Profit and Loss Account for the years ending 31 December 19X3 and 31 December 19X4 and the entries in the Balance Sheet as at 31 December 19X4.

TRADING ACCOUNT (p. 64)

98 What is the purpose of a Trading Account?

99 How would you define 'Gross Profit'?

100 What items would you expect to find included in a Trading Account?

101 Show how the following information would be recorded in the Trading Account of a business (show in vertical form).

Purchases	£3,000
Sales	9,000
Opening Stock	1,000
Closing Stock	1,500
Carriage Inwards	500
Sales Returns	300
Purchases Returns	200

The financial year ends on 31 December.

102 The following information relates to the trading results of B. Jones for year ended 31 December:

Opening Stock	£2,000
Purchases	5,000
Sales	8,000
Closing Stock	3,000

Prepare the Journal Entries to transfer the balances on the above Accounts to the Trading Account.

PROFIT AND LOSS ACCOUNT (p.68)

103 What is the purpose of a Profit and Loss Account?

104 Explain the method used to close Ledger accounts to the Profit and Loss Account.

105 What is the advantage of classifying expenses in the Profit and Loss Account?

106 W. White has balances on the following ledger accounts at 31 December which is his financial year end:

Trading Account (Cr) £8,000; Salaries (Dr) £1,000; Expenses (Dr) £2,000; Rates (Dr) £500; Commission Received (Cr) £300; Capital (Cr) £9,000. Rates due and unpaid at 31 December amounted to £200.

Show the entries in the above ledger accounts and close them off to the Profit and Loss Account. Prepare a Profit and Loss Account in ledger form. No journal entries are required.

107 From the following lists of balances extracted from B. Young's Trial Balance prepare his Profit and Loss Account in vertical form classifying the expenses under suitable headings:

Trial Balance (Extract) at 31 December

	Dr.	Cr.
Trading Account — Gross Profit		£10,000
Rent and Rates	£400	
Discount Allowed	100	
Audit Fees	80	
Advertising	70	
Salesmen's Salaries	3,000	
Office Salaries	2,000	
Telephone	150	
Bad Debts	40	
Heat & Light	200	
Bank Overdraft Interest	90	
Commission Received		300
General Office Expenses	120	

BALANCE SHEET (p.74)

108 What information does a Balance Sheet reveal to a businessman?

109 What is the difference between Fixed Assets and Current Assets?

110 What does the term 'Owner's Capital' mean in a Balance Sheet?

111 Distinguish between 'Long-term Liabilities' and 'Current Liabilities'.

112 From the following list of Assets and Liabilities record them under the appropriate headings (Fixed Assets, Current Assets, Current Liabilities and Long Term Liabilities) in order of permanence:

Freehold Property	£7,000	Debtors	£2,000
Mortgage	3,000	Plant	500
Stock of Goods	1,000	Motor Van	1,300
Creditors	400	Cash in Hand	100
Bank Overdraft	300	Fixtures and Fittings	700
Loan from X (Repayable in six months)	800	Prepaid Charge	50

113 The following balances were extracted from the books of A. Kane at 31 December:

Freehold Premises	£10,000
Stock of Goods	5,500
Capital — A. Kane 1 January	14,700
Debtors	2,000
Creditors	1,000
Motor Van	1,500
Bank Overdraft	3,000
Office Fixtures	2,500
Personal Drawings	4,000
Profit for Year	7,000

Prepaid Charge		300		
Accrued Charge		100		

You are required to prepare A.Kane's Balance Sheet at 31 December set out in such a manner as to show clearly the totals normally shown in a balance sheet.

114 A sole trader has prepared the following Balance Sheet:

Balance Sheet for Year ended 31 December

Bank Overdraft	£1,200	Personal Drawings	£4,000
Creditors	2,000	Stock	3,000
Discount Received	100	Plant	1,000
Provision for Doubtful	200	Debtors	3,900
Debts		Discount Allowed	50
Profit for Year	5,000	Cash	100
Capital at start of Year	8,000	Bad Debts	450
		Premises	4,000
	£16,500		£16,500

You are required to:
a) Correct the figure of profit shown in the Balance Sheet.
b) Redraft the above statement and prepare a Balance Sheet in vertical form.

BANK RECONCILIATION STATEMENT (p.80)

115 What is the purpose in preparing a Bank Reconciliation Statement?

116 Why can Cash Books and their related Bank Statements differ in content?

117 On 31 December 19X8 J. Black's Cash Book showed a balance of £200 representing cash at bank. At that date the cashier checked the bank statement received from the bank with the Cash Book and all the amounts agreed with the exception of the following:
   (a) Cheques received and paid into the Bank but not yet entered on the bank statement £400.
   (b) Cheques drawn and entered in the Cash Book but not yet presented to the Bank for payment £600.
   (c) Bank charges made by the Bank but not entered in the Cash Book £30.

The balance at bank shown in the bank statement at 31 December 19X8 was £370.

You are required to prepare a Bank Reconciliation Statement at 31 December 19X8.

118 The Bank Statement and Cash Book of J. Smith for May 19X7 are shown below:

Bank Statement

	Dr.	Cr.	Balance
May 1 Balance			£ 150
3 Lodgment		£80	230
5 Cheque 107	£50		180
10 Lodgment		100	280
15 Cheque 109	40		240
19 Cheque 108	20		220
25 Charges	10		210
28 Standing Order	5		205
30 Div. Received		30	235

CASH BOOK

DR							CR
Date	Details	Bank	Date	Details	Ch. No.	Bank	
May 1	Balance	£150	May 2	J. Brown	107	£50	
			8	W. Fox	108	20	
2	Sales	80					
			17	R. Jones	109	40	
10	Sales	100	28	Rent	S.O.	5	
			30	H. Green	110	70	
			31	Balance		145	
		£330				£330	

You are required to:

(a) Identify the reasons for the different balances at 31 May 19X7.

(b) Adjust J. Smith's Cash Book; and

(c) Prepare a Bank Reconciliation statement.

VALUE ADDED TAX (p.84)

119　List the information you would expect to see on an invoice involving V.A.T.

120　Show the rulings for a Cash Book which would be suitable for recording V.A.T. Enter a few transactions in the Cash Book to illustrate its use. No additional columns for discount and cash need be shown.

121　J. Smith has the following transactions in June:

June 7 Bought 2 cameras on credit from J. Down £115 (inc. V.A.T. £15)

　　　12 Returned 1 camera as faulty to J. Down £46 (inc V.A.T. £6)

V.A.T. rate is assumed to be 15%.

You are required to record these transactions in the books of J. Smith.

122 A. Deans has the following transactions in May:

May 9 Sold 10 cabinets on credit to W. Blue £345 (inc. V.A.T. £45)
    16 W. Blue returned one cabinet as damaged £23 (inc. V.A.T. £3)
You are required to record these transactions in the books of A. Deans.
Assume V.A.T. rate 15%.

123 From the following information prepare the V.A.T. Account as it would
appear in the books of D. Flax:

	V.A.T.
Total from Purchases Day Book	£ 98
Sales Day Book	205
Sales Returns Book	15
Purchases Returns Book	30
Cash Book (Tax on payments)	40
Cash Book (Tax on income)	20

These amounts related to the month of May.

ADDITIONAL QUESTIONS

I The following information has been extracted from the books of H. Bates
as at 31 December 19X2.

	Dr.	Cr.
General Office Expenses	£760	
Interest	1,400	
J. Jones — Loan		£16,000
Debtors	41,000	
Bank		5,000
Discount Allowed	1,272	
Bad Debts	296	
Petty Cash Balance	80	
Advertising	7,228	
Carriage Inwards	432	
Carriage Outwards	632	
H. Bates — Capital — 1 January 19X2		13,500
H. Bates — Drawings	2,076	
Office Fittings	2,400	
Provision for Depreciation		
Office Fittings		480
Showroom Equipment		300
Purchases	70,200	
Lighting	540	
Showroom Equipment	1,100	
Posts, Stationery and Telephone	600	
Stock — 1 January 19X2	14,268	
Insurance	360	

Provision for Doubtful Debts		800
Returns Outwards		2,280
Rent	1,600	
Creditors		10,136
Sales		111,020
Salesmen's Salaries	10,804	
Office Salaries	2,468	
	£159,516	£159,516

You are given the following additional information:
(a) Stock on Hand at 31 December 19X2 £14,000.
(b) The following amounts are due and unpaid at 31 December 19X2:

Telephone	£ 70
Rent	£300

(c) Provide for doubtful debts at £700.
(d) Depreciation is to be charged on office fittings and showroom equipment at 10% per annum on written down value.

You are required to prepare a Trading, Profit and Loss Account for year ended 31 December 19X2 and a Balance Sheet as at that date.

II   A. Bacon commenced business on 1 January 19X4 and his transactions were:

Jan 1	Capital Paid in and Lodged in Bank	£1,000
2	Purchased Machine by cheque	200
5	Purchased Goods from A. Blue on credit	150
6	Purchased Goods on credit from A. Brown	65
6	Paid Rent by cheque	30
7	Sold Goods to T. White on credit	40
8	Paid A. Blue by cheque (Discount Received £3)	147
10	Purchased from B. Thom goods on credit	120
11	Sold goods to H. Brand on credit	90
	Sold goods to W. Smith on credit	75
12	Paid A. Brown by cheque	65
13	Cash sale	15
13	Drawn from Bank for cash	40
14	Paid wages in cash	32
	Paid Petty Expenses in cash	5
15	Cash Purchases	3
	Sold goods on credit to T. Fowler	37
	Returned goods to B. Thom as faulty	20
16	E. Grant returned goods as damaged	50
	Purchased from A. Blue goods on credit	25
18	Received cash from T. White (Discount allowed £1)	39

20	Received cheque from H. Brand and lodged it in Bank	90
25	Cash Sale	7
27	Drawn from Bank for cash	35
31	Paid wages in cash	31
	Lodged in Bank from cash	30

You are required to write up the Books for the month of January and extract a Trial balance at 31 January.

III T. Horne commenced business on 1 January and introduced as his capital the following assets: Motor Van £1,000 and Stock of Goods £2,000. He paid £500 into the business bank account.

During the month of January the following transactions took place:

Jan 2 A cheque was drawn for cash £250.
  6 Bought goods on credit from T. Thom £350.
  8 Paid for a machine by cheque £250.
     Sold goods to R. Trott on credit £500 less trade discount 20%.
  9 Paid wages in cash £15.
 10 Cash sales £270.
 13 Bought goods on credit from W. Gray £700.
 14 Received cheque less 5% discount from R. Trott.
 15 Paid T. Thom amount due to him less 2½% discount.
 17 Paid rent by cheque £30.
 21 Returned goods to W. Gray £50.
 22 Sold goods to R. Short on credit £80.
 23 Bought goods on credit from J. Fife £100.
 24 R. Short returned damaged goods £5.
 25 Paid for shop fittings by cheque £200.
 31 Paid sundry expenses in cash £10.
     Paid into Bank from office cash £50.

You are required to:
(a) Record the above transactions in the Books of T. Horne.
(b) Make the following adjustments at 31 January.
        (i) Accrue Wages £10
        (ii) Prepay Rent £20
        (iii) Depreciate Van by £50.
        (iv) R. Short was declared bankrupt and the balance of his account had to be written off as bad.
        (v) Stock at end of January amounts to £2,500.
(c) Close off the books at 31 January and prepare a Trading and Profit and Loss Account for the month and a Balance Sheet as at 31 January.
Workings to nearest £.

Glossary of Accounting Terms

Glossary

The following are some of the more common accounting terms which are defined in abbreviated form.

Account
A record in the books of each aspect of every business transaction.

Accounting
The method of identifying, recording, measuring and reporting of financial information.

Accounting Period
The period of time covered by the final accounts of a business.

Accrued Charges
These are expenses which have been incurred for the period but have not been paid or recorded in the books within that period.

Assets
Items of value usually of a tangible nature.

Bad Debt
A bad debt arises when the debtor fails to pay either the whole, or part, of the debt.

Balance
The difference between two sides of an account.

Balance Sheet
A financial statement which shows the assets and liabilities of a business and the amount of owner's capital invested.

Books of Original Entry
The books into which transactions are first recorded.

Capital
The investment by the owner of a business which represents the excess of assets over liabilities.

Cash Book (Three column)
This book records receipts and payments made in cash or by cheque and also includes columns to record discount.

Cash Book (Two column)
This book records receipts and payments made in cash or by cheque.

Cash Discount
An allowance offered to customers as an encouragement for them to settle their debts promptly.

Contra Entries	Amounts transferred between two accounts e.g. cash paid to bank in the cash book.
Credit Entry	An entry on the right hand side of a ledger account.
Credit Note	A document sent by the seller of the goods to the buyer advising that his account has been credited and stating the amount and reasons for this credit.
Creditor	A person to whom money is owed.
Current Assets	These are assets which are constantly turning over in the day-to-day operations of the business.
Current Liabilities	These are liabilities which are settled within a short period of time.
Debit Entry	An entry on the left hand side of a ledger account.
Debtor	A person who owes money.
Depreciation	The loss in value of a fixed asset over a period of time.
Double-entry Accounting	The system of accounting where two entries are made for every transaction viz. debit entry and credit entry.
Final Accounts	These comprise the Trading and Profit and Loss Accounts and Balance Sheet.
Fixed Assets	These are made up of assets which are likely to remain in the business over a long period.
Folio	This is a page reference in an accounting book.
Impersonal Ledger	This book records real and nominal accounts and any other accounts which are not included in the sales or purchases ledgers.

Imprest Amount	A fixed sum of money which is held by the petty cashier out of which are made small cash payments. At the end of each week or month the amount expended is reimbursed to make it up to the fixed sum.
Invoice	A document sent by the seller of goods or services to the buyer giving details of the goods purchased, amount, quantity, terms, etc.
Journal	This book is used to record transactions which cannot be entered in a book of original entry before being posted to the ledger.
Journal Entry	This is recorded in the journal and indicates which account is to be debited and which account credited followed by a narrative explaining the nature of the transaction.
Ledger	Accounts are written up in this book.
Liabilities	Amounts owed by a business.
Lodgment	A sum of cash and/or cheques deposited in a Bank Account
Long-term Liabilities	These are amounts advanced to a business on a long term basis.
Nominal Accounts	Accounts recording items of income and expenditure.
Personal Accounts	Accounts of persons, firms and companies.
Petty Cash Book	This is a subsidiary cash book and is used to record small cash transactions.
Posting	The operation of transferring entries from books of original entry to the ledger or between ledger accounts.
Prepaid Charges	These are expenses which have been paid before the expiration of the period to which they relate.
Profit and Loss Account	This account is prepared to calculate the profit or loss for a period of trading.

Provision for Bad Debts	An amount set aside for anticipated losses caused by debtors failing to pay the full sum due by them.
Purchases Day Book	This book records and analyses all purchases for goods and services supplied on credit.
Purchases Ledger	This book records details of the personal aspects of all transactions affecting supplies of goods and services on credit.
Purchases Ledger Account	It is a simple and effective technique to control the arithmetical accuracy of the postings from the books of original entry to the Purchases Ledger.
Purchases Returns Book	This book records returns of goods bought on credit (sometimes referred to as returns outwards)
Real Accounts	Accounts which are tangible in nature e.g. Plant Account.
Returns Inwards	See Sales Returns Book.
Returns Outwards	See Purchases Returns Book.
Revenue Expenses	These are amounts spent by a business from which the benefit has been consumed during the accounting period e.g. Electricity and Rent.
Revenue Income	These are amounts of sales and other income the business has received.
Sales Day Book	This book records all sales of goods and services sold on credit.
Sales Ledger	This book records details of the personal aspects of all sales of goods and services on credit.
Sales Ledger Control Account	It is a simple and effective technique to control the arithmetical accuracy of the postings from the books of original entry to the Sales Ledger.
Sales Returns Book	This book records returns of goods sold on credit (sometimes referred to as returns inwards).

Stock	This represents purchases of goods for resale which have been made by a business and which have not been sold.
Suspense Account	An account which is used to record any items which cannot be posted to the proper ledger account because of lack of information at the time of the entry.
Trade Discount	An allowance given by the seller of goods to the buyer which is deducted from the gross amount of the sale in the invoice.
Trading Account	This account is prepared to calculate the gross profit for each accounting period.
Transaction	A business transaction is any exchange or transfer of goods or services which has a money value.
Trial Balance	This is a statement in which are listed debit and credit balances extracted from the ledger.
Value Added Tax	This is in principle chargeable on all supplies of goods and services in the United Kingdom by a taxable person in the course of their business. These goods and services are normally chargeable at the standard rate of V.A.T. which is currently 15%.

Examples of Accounting Documents

Example of Purchase Invoice sent by W. Smith to A. Draper

② W. Smith

MANUFACTURER
WOOLTOWN

INVOICE

No 350 **①**

A. Draper **④**
10 Cotton Street
Coaltown

③ Terms: 5% Discount 7 Days

⑤ 15 June 19

Quantity	Details	Amount
10	Suits @ £30 each **⑥** Less: Trade Discount 33 1/3%	£300.00 100.00
		£200.00 **⑦**

Key for Invoices

①   Invoice Number
②   Supplier
③   Settlement Terms
④   Purchaser
⑤   Invoice Date
⑥   Details of Purchase
⑦   Invoice Total

Examples of Sales Invoice sent by A. Draper to D. Stewart

A.DRAPER ❷

INVOICE

No 81 ❶

10, Cotton Street, Coaltown.

D. Stewart ❹
5 Satin Street
Wooltown

❸ Terms: 5% Discount 7 days

❺ 20 June 19

Quantity	Details	Amount
5	Shirts @ £6 ❻	£30.00
	Less: Trade Discount 30%	9.00
		£21.00 ❼

Example of Credit Note sent by W. Smith to A. Draper

❷ **W.Smith**

MANUFACTURER
WOOLTOWN

CREDIT NOTE

No 56 ❶

A. Draper ❸
10 Cotton Street
Coaltown

❹ 18 June 19

Quantity	Details	Amount
1	Suit Returned Faulty @ £30 ❺	£30.00
	Less: Trade Discount 33 1/3%	10.00
		£20.00 ❻

Key for Credit Notes

❶ Credit Note Number
❷ Supplier
❸ Purchaser
❹ Credit Note Date
❺ Details of Returns
❻ Credit Note Total

Example of Credit Note sent by A. Draper to D. Stewart

A.DRAPER ❷

CREDIT NOTE

No 72 ❶

10, Cotton Street, Coaltown.

D. Stewart ❸
5 Satin Street
Wooltown

❹ 25 June 19

Quantity	Details	Amount
1	Shirt @ £6 - damaged ❺	£6.00
	Less: Trade Discount 30%	1.80
		£4.20 ❻

Example of cheque

		90:12:252
17 June 19 —	**NEW BANK OF SCOTLAND**	
R. Brown	Head Office, Glasgow	*17ᵗʰ June* 19 —

Pay *R. Brown*   or order

Eighty Pounds.   £ *80 — 00*

A. Draper   *A. Draper*

315260   ⑈0╏295600 ⫶9b5E⚋0b ⣿09259E⫶

Example of pay-in slip

Current Account Pay-in
Acknowledgement

**NEW BANK
OF SCOTLAND**

Teller's
date stamp
and initials

Current Account Pay-in		Notes over £1	*100*	*00*
NEW BANK OF SCOTLAND		£1 Notes	*50*	*00*
Head Office, Glasgow		50p	*4*	*00*
Teller's		Silver	*2*	*00*
date stamp		Bronze	*1*	*00*
and initials	Date *8 July 19 —*	**Total Cash**	*1 57*	*00*
	Paid by *A Draper*	Cheques etc. (See over for details)	*70*	*00*
	Credit	**Total**	*227*	*00*

Total   *227 — 00*

Credit   *A DRAPER*

Name and A/c No   *A. Draper 00956210*

Subject to verification of
items other than cash

90:18

Example of Petty Cash Voucher

Petty Cash Voucher	No 4

Details	Amount
OFFICE TEA	*£1·00*

Signed   *B. Box*
Authorised   *A. Draper*

130

Quick Guide to Accounting Entries Index

Quick Guide to Accounting Entries

This guide covers the more important transactions which arise in business.

How to use this section of the book
Step 1 Select transaction.
    2 Check guide and select appropriate entries.
    3 Follow instructions and record transaction in books.

Example

Step 1
Transaction
On June 1 A. Draper introduced £1,000 by cheque as his capital.

Step 2
Entries from Check Guide

Debit Side	Credit Side
❶ Cash Book	*Ledger* Impersonal
❷ Bank/Cash Column	❺ *Account* Capital
❸ *Narrative* Capital	❻ *Narrative* Bank/Cash

Step 3
Recording transaction in Books

❶ Cash Book (Debit Side)   **(CB1)**

Date	Narrative	Folio	Discount Allowed	Cash	Bank
June 1	Capital ❸	$\frac{IL}{1}$			❷ £1,000

Impersonal Ledger ❹

DR   **Capital Account**   **(Folio 1)**   **CR**

				Date	Narrative	Folio	Amount
				June 1	Bank ❻	$\frac{CB}{1}$	£1,000

Instructions on left hand side represent debit entries and those on right hand side credit entries.

Day Books

Purchase on credit (e.g. Purchased goods on credit from J. Smith)
Ref: Page 12

Ledger:	Impersonal		*Ledger:*	Purchases	
Account:	Purchases		*Account:*	Name of Creditor	
Narrative:	Total from P.D.B.			(e.g. J. Smith)	
			Narrative:	Purchases	

Note: Each transaction must be entered in Purchases Day Book separately and only the total posted to the Purchases Account.

Sale on credit (e.g. Sold goods on credit to J. Jones)
Ref: Page 14

Ledger	Sales		*Ledger*	Impersonal	
Account	Name of Debtor		*Account*	Sales	
	(e.g. J. Jones)		*Narrative*	Total from S.D.B.	
Narrative	Sales				

Note: Each transaction must be entered in Sales Day Book separately and only the total posted to the Sales Account.

Purchases Returns or (Returns Outwards)
(e.g. Returned goods to J. Smith damaged)
Ref: Page 16

Ledger	Purchases		*Ledger*	Impersonal	
Account	Name of Creditor		*Account*	Purchases Returns or	
	(e.g. J. Smith)			Returns Outwards	
Narrative	Returns		*Narrative*	Total from P.R.B.	

Note: Each transaction must be entered in Purchases Returns Book separately and only the total posted to the Purchases Returns Account.

Sales Returns or (Returns Inwards) (e.g. J. Jones returned goods faulty)
Ref: Page 18

Ledger	Impersonal		*Ledger*	Sales
Account	Sales Returns or		*Account*	Name of Debtor
	Returns Inwards			(e.g. J. Jones)
Narrative	Total from S.R.B.		*Narrative*	Returns

Note: Each transaction must be entered in Sales Returns Book separately and only the total posted to the Sales Returns Account.

Cash Book - Receipts

Cheque/Cash introduced by owner as capital
(e.g. A Draper introduced £1,000 by cheque as capital)
Ref: Page 20

Cash Book			*Ledger*	Impersonal
Bank/Cash Column			*Account*	Capital
Narrative	Capital		*Narrative*	**Bank**/Cash

Cheque/Cash received from debtor (e.g. J. Jones paid his account by cheque)
Ref: Page 20

Cash Book			*Ledger*	Sales
Bank/Cash Column			*Account*	Name of Debtor
Narrative	Debtor's name			(e.g. J. Jones)
	(e.g. J. Jones)		*Narrative*	**Bank**/Cash

Cheque/Cash received from debtor with discount allowed
(e.g. J. Jones paid his account by cheque £100 discount allowed £5.)
Ref: Page 22

Cash Book			*Ledger*	Sales
Bank/Cash Column (£100)			*Account*	Name of Debtor
Discount allowed shown in				(e.g. J. Jones)
Discount Column (£5)			*Narrative*	**Bank**/Cash (£100)
Narrative	Debtor's name			Discount Allowed (£5)
	(e.g. J. Jones)			

Note: Total of discount allowed column is posted to 'DR' of Discount Allowed Account.

Cash Sale (e.g. Cash Sales for month £500)
Ref: Page 20

Cash Book Cash Column *Narrative* Sales	*Ledger* Impersonal *Account* Sales or Cash Sales *Narrative* Cash

Cash transfer to Bank (contra entry) (e.g. £50 cash paid into Bank)
Ref: Page 20

Cash Book Bank Column *Narrative* Cash	Cash Book Cash Column *Narrative* Bank

Cheque/Cash—Capital Receipt (e.g. Proceeds from sale of asset *or* receipt of a loan)
Ref: Page 20

Cash Book **Bank**/Cash Column *Narrative* Name of Account (e.g. Asset A/c or Loan A/c)	*Ledger* Impersonal *Account* Name of Account (e.g. Asset A/c or Loan A/c) *Narrative* **Bank**/Cash

Cheque/Cash — Revenue Income (e.g. Commission received £10)
Ref: Page 20

Cash Book **Bank**/Cash Column *Narrative* Name of Income Account (e.g. Commission A/c)	*Ledger* Impersonal *Account* Name of Income Account (e.g. Comm- ission A/c) *Narrative* **Bank**/Cash

For Summary of Revenue Income items see Trial Balance list page 47

Cash Book –Payments

Cheque/Cash paid to creditor (e.g. Paid J. Smith amount due £100)
Ref: Page 20

Ledger Purchases *Account* Name of Creditor (e.g. J. Smith) *Narrative* **Bank**/Cash	Cash Book **Bank**/Cash Column *Narrative* Name of Creditor (e.g. J. Smith)

Cheque/Cash paid to creditor with discount received
(e.g. Paid J. Smith his account £100 by cheque discount received £5.)
Ref: Page 22

Ledger	Purchases	Cash Book
Account	Name of Creditor	Bank/Cash Column (£100)
	(e.g. J. Smith)	Discount Received shown in
Narrative	Bank/Cash (£100)	Discount column.
	Discount Received (£5)	*Narrative* Name of Creditor
		(e.g. J. Smith)

Note: Total of discount received column is posted to 'CR' of Discount Received Account.

Cash Purchase (e.g. Cash Purchases for month £200)
Ref: Page 20

Ledger	Impersonal	Cash Book
Account	Purchases or Cash	Cash Column
	Purchases	*Narrative* Purchases
Narrative	Cash	

Cash transfer from Bank (contra entry) (e.g. £100 drawn from bank for cash)
Ref: Page 22

Cash Book	Cash Book
Cash Column	Bank Column
Narrative Bank	*Narrative* Cash

Cheque/Cash for Capital Expenditure
(e.g. Purchased motor car by cheque £2,000)
Ref: Page 20

Ledger	Impersonal	Cash Book
Account	Name of Capital	Bank/Cash Column
	Expenditure Account	*Narrative* Name of Capital
	(e.g. Motor Car)	Expenditure Account
Narrative	Bank/Cash	(e.g. Motor Car)

For summary of Capital Expenditure see Assets in Trial Balance list page 47

Cheque/Cash for Revenue Expenditure (e.g. Paid wages by cheque £100)
Ref: Page 20

Ledger	Impersonal	Cash Book	
Account	Name of Revenue	Bank/Cash Column	
	Expenditure Account	Narrative	Name of Revenue
	(e.g. Wages)		Expenditure Account
Narrative	Bank/Cash		(e.g. Wages)

For summary of Revenue Expenditure see Trial Balance list page 47.

Cash transfer to Petty Cash (e.g. Transfer to Petty Cash Book £30)
Ref: Page 26

Petty Cash Book	Cash Book	
Cash Column	Cash Column	
Narrative Cash	Narrative Petty Cash	

Cheque/Bank—Personal Drawings of Owner
(e.g. Owner drew cash for own use £50)
Ref: Page 20

Ledger	Impersonal	Cash Book	
Account	Personal Drawings	Bank/Cash Column	
Narrative	Bank/Cash	Narrative Drawings	

Dishonoured cheque from debtor (e.g. J. Jones cheque for £100 was dishonoured)

Ledger	Sales	Cash Book	
Account	Debtor's Account	Bank column	
	(e.g. J. Jones)	Narrative	Debtor's name who
Narrative	Bank		dishonoured cheque
			(e.g. J. Jones)

Adjustments in Ledger Accounts

Accrued Charge (e.g. Wages accrued at end of period £20)
Ref: Page 54

Ledger	Impersonal		*Ledger*	Impersonal
Account	Revenue Expense		*Account*	Revenue Expense
	'old' account			'new' account
	(e.g. Wages)			(e.g. Wages)
Narrative	Accrued		*Narrative*	Accrued

Note: This adjustment must be recorded through Journal before posting to Ledger.

Prepaid Charge (e.g. Insurance prepaid at end of period £15)
Ref: Page 52

Ledger	Impersonal		*Ledger*	Impersonal
Account	Revenue Expense		*Account*	Revenue Expense
	'new' account			'old' account
	(e.g. Insurance)			(e.g. Insurance)
Narrative	Prepaid		*Narrative*	Prepaid

Note: This adjustment must be recorded through the Journal before posting to Ledger.

Bad Debt written off (e.g. J. Jones account £100 written off as bad)
Ref: Page 56

Ledger	Impersonal		*Ledger*	Sales
Account	Bad Debts		*Account*	Name of Debtor
Narrative	Name of Debtor			(e.g. J. Jones)
	(e.g.J. Jones)		*Narrative*	Bad Debts

Note: This adjustment must be recorded through the Journal before posting to Ledger.

Bad Debt Recovered (Payment by cheque)
(e.g. Recovered from J. Jones whose debt had been written off as bad £20)

Cash Book		*Ledger*	Impersonal
Bank Column		*Account*	Bad Debts Recovered
Narrative	Bad Debt Recovered	*Narrative*	Bank

Bad Debts Provision (e.g. make a bad debts provision of 5% of debtors)
Ref: Page 58

Ledger	Impersonal	*Ledger*	Impersonal
Account	Profit and Loss Account	*Account*	Provision for Bad Debts
Narrative	Provision for Bad Debts	*Narrative*	Profit and Loss

Note: This adjustment must be recorded through the Journal before posting to Ledger.

Depreciation of Fixed Assets (e.g. Write off 10% Depreciation from Fixtures)
Ref: Page 60

Ledger	Impersonal	*Ledger*	Impersonal
Account	Depreciation	*Account*	Asset Account (e.g. Fixtures)
Narrative	Name of Asset Account (e.g. Fixtures)	*Narrative*	Depreciation

Notes: 1. Depreciation can be posted to a separate account known as 'Provision for Depreciation Account' instead of being credited to the asset account.
2. This adjustment must be recorded through the Journal before posting to the Ledger.

Opening Entries

Capital introduced by owner where more than one asset is involved
(e.g. A. Draper commenced business with Stock £500, Motor Car £1,000 and
Cash £100 as his capital)
Ref: Page 76

Ledger	Impersonal and Cash Book	*Ledger*	Impersonal
Account	Accounts relating to assets introduced as capital (e.g. Stock, Motor Car and Cash)	*Account*	Capital
Narrative	Capital	*Narrative*	Sundries

Notes: 1. The narrative 'Sundries' is used in the Capital Account since more
than one account is involved and only the total is shown in that
account.
2. This adjustment must be recorded through the Journal before posting
to Ledger.

Closing Entries

Opening Stock transferred to Trading Account
Ref: Page 64

Ledger	Impersonal	*Ledger*	Impersonal
Account	Trading	*Account*	Stock
Narrative	Stock	*Narrative*	Trading

This adjustment must be recorded through the Journal before posting to Ledger.

Closing Stock transferred to Trading Account
Ref: Page 64

Ledger	Impersonal	*Ledger*	Impersonal
Account	Stock	*Account*	Trading
Narrative	Trading	*Narrative*	Stock

This adjustment must be recorded through the Journal before posting to Ledger.

Purchases and Sales Returns transferred to Trading Account
Ref: Page 64

Ledger Account Narrative	Impersonal Trading Purchases or Sales Returns	Ledger Account Narrative	Impersonal Purchases or Sales Returns Trading

Notes: 1. Any other expense item which required to be transferred to Trading Account would be treated in same way e.g. Carriage Inwards.
2. This adjustment must be recorded through the Journal before posting to Ledger.

Sales and Purchases Returns transferred to Trading Account
Ref: Page 64

Ledger Account Narrative	Impersonal Sales or Purchases Returns Trading	Ledger Account Narrative	Impersonal Trading Sales or Purchases Returns

This adjustment must be recorded through the Journal before posting to Ledger.

Gross Profit for period transferred to Profit and Loss Account
Ref: Page 68

Ledger Account Narrative	Impersonal Trading Profit and Loss	Ledger Account Narrative	Impersonal Profit and Loss Trading

This adjustment must be recorded through the Journal before posting to the Ledger.

Revenue Expenditure items transferred to Profit and Loss Account
Ref: Page 68

Ledger Account Narrative	Impersonal Profit and Loss Name of Expenses Account (e.g. Wages)	Ledger Account Narrative	Impersonal Name of Expenses Account (e.g. Wages) Profit and Loss

Notes: 1. For Revenue Expenditure items see Trial Balance list page 47.
2. This adjustment must be recorded through the Journal before posting to Ledger.

Revenue Income items transferred to Profit and Loss Account
Ref: Page 68

Ledger	Impersonal	*Ledger*	Impersonal
Account	Name of Income	*Account*	Profit and Loss
	Account	*Narrative*	Name of Income
	(e.g. Discount Received)		Account (e.g.
Narrative	Profit and Loss		Discount Received)

Notes: 1. For Revenue Income items see Trial Balance list page 47.
2. This adjustment must be recorded through the Journal before posting to the Ledger.

Profit or Loss for the period transferred to Capital Account
Ref: Page 68

Ledger	Impersonal	*Ledger*	Impersonal
Account	Profit and Loss	*Account*	Capital
Narrative	Capital	*Narrative*	Profit and Loss

Notes: 1. If a loss arises the entries are reversed.
2. This adjustment must be recorded through the Journal before posting to Ledger.

Personal Drawings transferred to Capital Account
Ref: Page 90/93/94

Ledger	Impersonal	*Ledger*	Impersonal
Account	Capital	*Account*	Personal Drawings
Narrative	Personal Drawings	*Narrative*	Capital

This adjustment must be recorded through the Journal before posting to the Ledger.

Answers to Questions

3.

Business Receives	Business Gives	
(a) Goods value £50	(a) Cash value	£50
(b) Rent value £30	(b) Cash value	£30
(c) Cash value £100	(c) Goods value	£100

7. Cash A/c Dr. Capital £2,500, Sales £600; Cr. Purchases £400,
   Rent £50, Wages £30, Motor Car £1,600.
   Capital A/c Cr. Cash £2,500.
   Purchases A/c Dr. Cash £400.
   Sales A/c Cr. Cash £600.
   Rent A/C Dr. Cash £50.
   Wages A/c Dr. Cash £30.
   Motor Car A/c Dr. Cash £1,600

10 R. Jack A/c Cr. Purchases £60; Purchases A/c Dr. R. Jack £60,
   B. Smart A/c Dr. Sales £90; Sales A/c Cr. B. Smart £90.

12 Closing balances brought down Cash A/c Dr. £820; Sales A/c Cr. £120;
   Purchases A/c Dr. £780.

14 Totals of debit and credit columns £715.

17 Plant — Asset; Debtors — Asset; Sales — Income; Wages — Expenses;
   Carriage — Expenses; Postage — Expenses; Creditors — Liability; Land —
   Asset and Discount Received — Income.

20 a) Revenue; b) Capital; c) Revenue; d) Capital; e) Revenue; f) Revenue.

22 (a) Personal; (b) Nominal; (c) Real; (d) Personal; (e) Real (f) Nominal.

28 Purchases Day Book total £353. Balances on Accounts: R. Smith Cr.
   £240; W. Wilson Cr. £65; J. Bryce Cr. £48; Purchases Dr. £353.

32 Sales Day Book total £675. Balances on Accounts: B. East Dr. £300;
   W. Green Dr. £240; N. Smart Dr. £135; Sales Cr. £675.

35   Purchases Returns Book total £124. Balances on Accounts: R. Smith
           Dr. £100; J. Bryce Dr. £24; Purchases Returns Cr. £124.
37   Sales Returns Book total £170. Balances on Accounts: W. Green Cr.
           £35; N. Smart Cr. £135; Sales Returns Dr. £170.
39   Cash Book balances: Cash Dr. £158; Bank Dr. £15.
40   Cash Book balances: Cash Dr. £30; Bank Dr. £130.
           Balances on Accounts: J. Smith Cr. £80; G. Green Dr. £90;
                                Interest Cr. £20; Wages Dr. £10.
43   Cash Book totals Dr. side — Discount £4, Cash £135, Bank £518
                      Cr. side — Discount £7, Cash £135, Bank £518.
           Closing balances brought down — Cash Dr. £96, Bank Dr. £325;
44   Cash book totals Dr. side — Discount £4; Cash £110; Bank £200.
           Cash Book totals Cr. side — Discount £5; Cash £110; Bank £200.
           Closing balances brought down — Cash Dr. £40; Bank Cr. £70.
           Ledger Account balances — J. Brown Cr. £84; D. Black Dr. £205;
              Interest Cr. £10; Wages Dr. £30; Discount Allowed Dr. £4; Discount
           Received Cr. £5.
46   Petty Cash Book totals Dr. side — Receipts £40; Cr. side total £40;
           Posts etc. £17; Travelling £7; Carriage £3; Office Expenses £2. Balance
           down £11.
48   Petty Cash Book totals Dr. Side — Receipts £68; Cr. Side Total
           £68; Postage £8; Carriage £4; Office Cleaning £12; Stationery
           £4; Balance brought down £40.
           Ledger Account balances: Cash Book Cr. £28; Postage Dr. £8; Carriage Dr.
           £4; Office Cleaning Dr. £12; Stationery Dr. £4.
51   Dr. Premises £1,500, Plant £200, Stock £300; Cr. Capital £2.000 Dr. Plant
           £600; Cr. G. Gray £600.
52   Dr. Trading £4,000; Cr. Purchases £4,000
           Dr. Sales £7,000;   Cr. Trading £7,000
           Dr. Trading £3,000 Cr. Profit and Loss £3,000 (Transfer of Gross Profit)
           Dr. Profit & Loss £1,000 Cr. Office Expenses £1,000
54   J. Smith A/c — Total both sides   £50
           W. Green A/c —   "   "   "   £70
           Purchases Day Book total   £120
           Purchases Returns Book total   £10
           Cash Book — Cr. Side — Discount £3, Bank £107.

56 D. Brown A/c — Total both sides £100.
    R. Black A/c —   ,,   ,,   ,,   £75.
    Sales Day Book total £175.
    Sales Returns Book total £20.
    Cash Book — Dr. Side — Discount £3; Bank £152.
59 Balance brought down Cr. £4,755
62 Balance brought down Dr. £3,570
66 Cash Book totals Dr. Side — Cash £35
       ,,   ,,   ,,   Cr. Side — Cash £5; Bank £130.
    Ledger Account Balances — Rates Dr. £50; Electricity Dr. £80.
    Purchases Dr. £5; Interest Cr. £20; Sales Cr. £15.
69 Balances brought down: June 1 Dr. £50; July 1 Dr. £15; August 1 Dr. £70.
73 Trial Balance totals £21,966
76 Suspense A/c Dr. B. Smith £70, Purchases £120, A. Black £5.
               Cr. Diff. in T.B. £60, Typewriter £135.
78 Stock A/c Dr. Balance £5,000; Trading £7,000.
           Cr. Trading £5,000.
    Trading A/c Dr. Stock £5,000; Cr. Stock £7,000.
    Balance Sheet — Current Assets — Stock £7,000.
81 Insurance A/c: Dr. Bank £200, Balance b/d £50
              Cr. Prepaid £50, Profit and Loss £150.
84 Rates A/c Dr. Bank £150, Bank £150, Bank £150, Accrued £150
             Cr. Profit and Loss £600, Balance b/d £150.
87 A. Blue A/c: Dr. Balance £50; Cr. Bad Debts £50.
    C. Green A/c: Dr. Balance £80; Cr. Bad Debts £80.
    Bad Debts A/c Dr. A. Blue £50, C. Green £80; Cr. Profit & Loss £130.
    Amount in Profit and Loss Account for Bad Debts is £130.

90 Journal: Dr. Profit and Loss £100; Cr. Provision for Bad Debts £100.
Provision for Bad Debts A/c: Cr. Profit and Loss £100.
Profit and Loss A/c: Dr. Provision for Bad Debts £100.
Balance Sheet: Debtors £2,000 less Provision for Bad Debts £100 =
£1,900.

94 Machine A/c Balance b/d Jan 1 19X4 Dr. £1,280. Profit and Loss A/c
19X2 — £400; 19X3 £400.
Balance Sheet 19X3: Machine £1,680 less Depn. £400 = £1,280.

97 Van A/c Balance b/d Jan. 1 19X5 Dr. £3,840.
Profit and Loss A/c: 19X3 — £1,200; 19X4 — £960.
Balance Sheet 19X4 Van £4,800 less Depreciation £960 = £3,840.

101 Gross Profit £5,900.

102 Journal: Dr. Trading £7,000; Cr. Purchases £5,000, Stock £2,000
           Dr. Sales £8,000; Cr. Trading £8,000
           Dr. Stock £3,000; Cr. Trading £3,000.

106 Capital A/c Dr. Balance £13,600; Cr. Balance £9,000 Profit and Loss
£4,600.
Profit and Loss A/c Dr. Salaries £1,000, Expenses £2,000, Rates £700,
Capital (Profit) £4,600; Cr. Trading £8,000, Commission £300.

107 Profit for Year £4,050.
(Admin. Expenses £2,950; Selling Expenses £3,110; Finance
Expenses £190.

112 Fixed Assets (Property £7,000, Plant £500, Van £1,300, Fittings £700).
Current Assets (Stock £1,000, Debtors £2,000, Prepaid £50, Cash £100).
Current Liabilities (Loan £800, Overdraft £300, Creditors £400). Long-
term Liabilities (Mortgage £3,000). Difference is Capital £8150.

113 Capital £17,700 + Liabilities £4,100 = £21,800
Fixed Assets £14,000 + Current Assets £7,800 = £21,800.

114 (a) Profit (5,000 + Disc. Received £100 — Bad Debts £450 — Discount
        Allowed £50) = *£4,600*
     (b) Fixed Assets £5,000 + Current Assets £6,800 — Current Liabilities
        £3,200 = £8,600.
        Capital (8,000 + 4,600 — 4,000) = *£8,600*

117 Adjusted Cash Book Balance (200 − 30) = *£170.*
   Adjusted Bank Statement Balance (370 + 400 − 600) = £170.
118 Adjusted Cash Book Balance (145 + 30 − 10) = *£165.*
   Adjusted Bank Statement Balance (235 − 70) = £165.
121 Purchase Day Book totals − Total £115, V.A.T. £15, Amount (Ex V.A.T.) £100.
   Purchase Returns Book totals − Total £46, V.A.T. £6, Amount (Ex V.A.T.) £40
   Ledger Account Balances: J. Down Dr. £46; Cr. £115.
                        Purchases Dr. £100.
                        Purchases Returns Cr. £40.
                        V.A.T. A/c Dr. £15; Cr. £6
122 Sales Day Book totals − Total £345, V.A.T. £45, Amount (Ex V.A.T.) £300.
   Sales Returns Book totals − Total £23, V.A.T. £3, Amount (Ex V.A.T.) £20.
   Ledger AccountBalances: W. Blue Dr. £345; Cr. £23.
                        Sales Cr. £300.
                        Sales Returns Dr. £20.
                        V.A.T. A/c Dr. £3; Cr. £45
123 V.A.T. A/c Dr. (98 + 15 + 40 + Balance 102) = £255.
            Cr. (30 + 205 + 20) = £255.